C000057223

ANGLICAN EVANGELICAL IDENTITY

Yesterday and Today

J. I. Packer & N. T. Wright

The Latimer Trust

REGENT COLLEGE PUBLISHING
Vancouver, British Columbia

Anglican Evangelical Identity
Copyright © 2008 J. I. Packer and N. T. Wright
All rights reserved.

This edition published 2009 by special arrangement with the
Latimer Trust
PO Box 26685
London N14 4XQ
www.latimertrust.org

Regent College Publishing
5800 University Boulevard
Vancouver, British Columbia
V6T 2E4 Canada
Web: www.regentpublishing.com
E-mail: info@regentpublishing.com

The studies in this volume were first published individually by Latimer House in Oxford. They are reprinted here without verbal amendment except to align page references within this publication, where the studies refer to each other. They are supplemented by new Prefaces by the Authors.

The original Latimer Studies were:

The Evangelical Anglican Identity Problem – an analysis by J. I. Packer, first published 1978, ISBN 0 946307 00 8

Evangelical Anglican Identity – The Connection between Bible, Gospel and Church by N. T. Wright, first published 1980, ISBN 0 946307 07 5

A Kind of Noah's Ark? The Anglican Commitment to Comprehensiveness by J. I. Packer, first published 1981, ISBN 0 946307 09 1

Views expressed in works published by Regent College Publishing are those of the author and do not necessarily represent the official position of Regent College (www.regent-college.edu).

ISBN 978-1-57383-428-5

A cataloguing record for this publication is available from Library and Archives Canada

Contents

Hz Biggs

Preface by Jim Packer (2008)

Luther told his critic Erasmus that he wrote to establish consciences, and that is what I was trying to do in the two occasional pieces of mine that are reprinted here. A Christian's conscience is that power of mind which, when enlightened by Scripture, the Holy Spirit, and full knowledge of the relevant facts, discerns and declares to us, in the manner of a monitor within, God's judgment on us and his directions to us. Establishing consciences means helping believers from uncertainty into clear certainty on any aspect of their ongoing relation to God about which they currently have doubts: where they stand with him, how and where they should be serving him, how to honour and please him in bewildering circumstances, and so forth. *The Evangelical Anglican Identity Problem* (1978) addressed Anglican evangelicals who were unsure whether it was warrantable to continue as Anglicans. *A Kind of Noah's Ark?* (1981) had in view clergy and laity who were baffled and discouraged by the continually broadening spectrum of tolerated unorthodoxies within the Church of England, and in particular the hesitations felt by young men called to be pastors who were unsure whether it made sense to pursue their vocation as Anglicans. Both pieces were thus tracts for the times.

When I wrote the first I was preparing to answer God's call to Canada, and when I wrote the second I was already teaching in Canada, so those two items were in effect my swan song to the Church of England. I had hoped, I confess, that the move might be a providentially orchestrated shift away from the burden of doctrinal distress and debate that had been mine for the two previous decades, but it proved not to be so; I found myself involved in the same problems, at some points in an acuter form. When I was asked to write this Preface, and say how I felt about the opinions I expressed so long ago, and whether I wished to qualify them or add to them in any way, I re-read both pieces, something I had not done for more than a quarter of a century, and found, not merely that the questions and arguments were still very much alive in my mind, but also that my mind had not changed on anything essential. How far evangelical consciences still need establishing in the way that I thought they did during my last months in England I am not sure. My impression is that in the Church of England evangelicals are both more numerous and more fragmented than they were when I left in 1979, and that uncertainty as to how to face up to the ongoing doctrinal disorder is less than it was, for people are more used to it and have already made at least provisional decisions about it. Whether or not I am right on that, however, I am happy to answer the questions that have been asked.

Do I still agree with what these pieces say? Yes. There is nothing in them that I would withdraw. Despite ongoing doctrinal and now moral deviations within Anglicanism, I continue an Anglican by reason of the theological and spiritual wealth of the Anglican heritage; I continue to encourage candidates for Anglican orders, and I direct what is in effect an ordination course within Regent College's transdenominational M.Div.; and I pray and work as best I can for worldwide Anglican repentance, reformation, renewal and revival, as needed. And I am hugely heartened by the black-and-white orthodoxy – biblical soundness, that is – of most of the Anglican world, outside what we may call the Old West (Britain, North America and Australasia): a glorious fact that has only broken surface within the last few years, but is clearly heavy with significance for the Anglican future.

Have I anything to add to what I wrote three decades ago? Yes. Things have moved on. Ideas have legs; they lead not only to talking, but to walking and taking action; and the attitudes and actions that the liberal unorthodoxy of the past half-century has now begotten are splitting the entire Anglican Communion in two. Two issues have come to be at stake; I will lay them out before making comments on them.

Blessing same-sex unions liturgically, in church, as if they were marriages, is the first issue. There is a history here. In 2002 the Bishop of New Westminster, at the request of a majority of his diocesan Synod (a request that he had in effect asked them to

2

make), committed the diocese to practise these blessings. Theologically and liturgically, this was to treat gay partnerships as holy vocations in God's sight. Representatives of several congregations, including myself, saw this as a major matter, and we at once declared ourselves out of communion with the Bishop and the Synod for their unconstitutional rejection, and indeed defiance, of four strands of authority; the biblical condemnation of gay behaviour; the gospel call to repentance and holiness, in the course of which homosexual behaviour is named as a sin that must be forsaken (1 Cor. 6:9-10); the strong verdict against homosexual practice given by the 1998 Lambeth Conference; and the tradition of pastoral help towards homosexual chastity, matching the pastoral help against fornication and adultery (masturbation, too) that all churches have been giving ever since Christianity began. Having stated our position, we walked out of the Synod; we constituted ourselves the Anglican Communion in New Westminster (ACiNW); we resolved to withhold funds from the diocese till it and the Bishop should backtrack; and we sought alternative episcopal oversight (AEO). (This did not however materialise.)

As the ripples of a stone thrown into a pond spread to its edges, so the ripples of these events, plus the subsequent consecration of an active homosexual as a bishop in the USA, have gone throughout the Anglican Communion. The upshot is that the canonical rule of convenience, dating from the fourth century, which forbids bishops to intrude into each other's geographical area of jurisdiction (i.e. their dioceses), has been breached; dozens of American parishes are now under African jurisdiction, and the ACiNV, in company with some American dioceses, is in process of coming under the jurisdiction of the Archbishop of the Southern Cone. Also, several separated episcopal bodies are planning a new, non-geographical, biblically orthodox province for North America extending across both the USA and Canada.. A majority of Anglican provinces are in impaired communion with North America. Major realignment is taking place, though within the Anglican fellowship, not away from it.

Seeking the convergence of all religions, displaying them as inwardly one and melding their separate traditions together, is the second issue at stake. Multi-faith occasions, seminary courses, and public affirmations of other faiths by Christian leaders, are mounted as steps toward this goal, with corresponding de-emphasis on the uniqueness of the Lord Jesus Christ and his solitariness as Saviour. Since, however, major institutional changes to further this process are not yet widespread, here we merely note that it exists, and has a considerable head of steam powering it.

Both these developments stem from the same source: a peculiarly virulent form of Protestant liberal theology which came to dominate North American theological schools in the 1960s, and still does. This liberalism knows nothing of a God who uses written human language to tell us things, or about the human fallenness that makes redemption necessary. This teaching posits, rather, a natural religiosity in man (regard, that is, for some higher power), and a natural capacity for goodwill and justice, and it sees the Christian church as a force for cherishing and canalizing these qualities, as the Jesus of history, restructured and desupernaturalized on liberal terms, is thought to have taught his disciples that they must do and teach others to do. Liberalism sees the world's emerging concerns as God's agenda for the church; so the church must constantly play catch-up to the culture, embracing as from God whatever is the "in-thing" at the moment (minority rights, including gay rights, for example), and thus showing the church to be alert and active in promoting human welfare. In following this agenda the church will inevitably leave the Bible behind at various points, but since on this view the Bible is the word of fallible men rather than of the infallible God, leaving it behind will be no great loss.

Once I thought liberalism was on its last legs, but now I know better. As mosquitoes invigorate themselves by sucking into themselves our blood, so liberalism renews itself by sucking into itself the concerns of the culture and reshaping its account of Christianity around them. However effectively its rationalistic critiques of God's supra-rational revelation of himself get answered, liberalism will always be renewing itself in the manner

4

described. We should budget for the fact that, like the poor, it will always be with us. But I cannot pursue this theme here.

The bottom line is that in today's situation I see reason and need to supplement what I urged in my tracts for the times, thirty years ago, with the following three maxims:

From now on, first, think *globally* rather than *domestically*. My original tracts centred upon appreciating the classic evangelical tradition in the Church of England, and did not look outside England at all. I do not think that was a fault, for I had set myself to establish consciences in relation to how that tradition was faring, and as I see it I was simply trying to do my job. Today, however, such thinking, if it stood alone, would be an unrealistic and unspiritual anachronism. During the past thirty years the Christian world, like the secular world, has shrunk into a single global village, which means that it has grown into an interconnected reality of which no part can be well thought about save in relation to the other parts. This is certainly true of Anglicanism. Nearly all the significant Anglican action, and specifically Anglican evangelical action, during the past generation has taken place outside Britain. The pentecostal-charismatic Spirit-centredness that has touched Anglicans, like others, all round the world was a global movement from the start. The task of developing everywhere indigenous yet transcultural versions of Anglican evangelicalism is everywhere recognized, and in it big strides have already been made. To be exclusively (for instance) England-centred in one's thoughts about evangelicalism at such a time would be so narrow and out of touch as to be actually Spirit-quenching. Which leads to my next point.

From now on, second, think of the *future* rather than the *past* – that is, think of the faithful Christian heritage as a springboard and resource to help achieve a faithful Christian future, rather than as a straitjacketing restraint upon it. Do not lapse into nostalgia! Living in the past snuffs out wisdom in the present, for wisdom in the present always has the future in view. "Say not, 'Why were the former days better than these?' For it is not from wisdom that you ask this" (Eccl. 6:10). The matter is one

5

of mindset. No one who lives in a faithful – faith-full, faith-filled – way under the providence of our sovereign God should feel threatened by the need for change, or the reality of change as God (yes, God, not just Satan) takes things forward. New situations, however perplexing and unhappy in the short term, should always be seen as new opportunities, calling us to new ventures in hopeful prayer and faith-filled obedience. The Anglican Communion, and the Church of England as part of it, is currently in the toils of internal re-alignment to maintain faithfulness, as we saw; every congregation in every diocese in the Old West faces pressures and problems rooted in the widening gap between what public law enacts and what Holy Scripture prescribes; and every person, young and old, in all our secular communities needs Jesus Christ as much as anyone ever did. Looking back to some supposed golden age and dreaming of reproducing it is not likely to help us to fulfil the calling that God gives us today, which of course includes planning for tomorrow. Things move on, and with God's help so must we. What we face is, precisely, a task – *our* task.

So from now on, third, think *theocentrically* rather than *institutionally*. Remember that God is always active, though institutions become static. Remember that under the new covenant God-centred thinking is Christ-centred and Spirit-centred no less than Creator-centred, and that the holy Three are at work as a team, bringing to reality the wonder of new creation. Think everything out, therefore, in terms of making our ongoing story, personal and congregational, in the diocese, the province, the global Anglican communion and the universal church militant here in earth, a real and evident part of God's ongoing story, namely the Triune project of calling, sanctifying, nurturing, purifying and perfecting, a multinational fellowship of individual believers destined for unending worship, service and joy together in a world yet to come. The narrative theology of recent decades, capsuled for us in N. T. Wright's contribution to this book (and magisterially expanded by him in many learned works since) shows us what God's story is, right up to its coming consummation, and it is for us to fit into this divine framework of love, wisdom, holiness and power. When and as this requires change, even

6

ecclesiastical restructuring and/or realignment, so be it. Idolizing the church, after all, betrays its Lord.

J.I.PACKER

JANUARY 2008

Preface by Tom Wright (2008)

One morning in late 1980 I was sitting at my desk in Downing College, Cambridge when the phone rang.

'Henry Chadwick speaking,' said a well-known Olympian voice.

My heart beat faster. What could a Regius Professor (he had moved to the Cambridge Chair after ten years as Dean of Christ Church) have to say to a young College Chaplain?

'I have just read your Latimer Study.'

Horrors. I guessed they'd sent it to him for review in the *Journal of Theological Studies*. But – if he was going to read something I'd written, why couldn't he have chosen one of my (admittedly scarce at that point) scholarly writings about Paul, rather than a hastily-written, popular-level tract for the times, designed for internal evangelical consumption? I was just bidding goodbye to any hope of being taken seriously as a theologian, when he continued,

'I just wanted to you to know that, if I were to say that I agreed with every word you wrote, I hope you would not take that as an indication that you must have made some terrible mistake somewhere.'

Incredulous, I spluttered the beginnings of an astonished 'thank you'. It wasn't necessary; he must have known the effect his words would have.

'That's all I wanted to say. Goodbye.'

I sat there, staring at the phone, trying to take in one of the greatest, and most unexpected, encouragements I have ever received.

I tell that story here, partly out of homage to a very great man, recently gone to his rest, to whom Evangelicals have not always realised their indebtedness, and partly to show that eager young Evangelicals may not always appreciate where some of their true friends are to be found. And also partly to introduce what I want to say upon reading Jim Packer's two booklets between which, to my surprise and delight, my own is now reprinted. Packer to right of me, Packer to left of me, volleying and thundering with the same acumen, wry humour, and clear, crisp, enjoyable prose: it brings back happy memories of the 1970s, not least when Jim was Chairman of Latimer House Council and I was its Secretary. And, speaking now from the opposite angle to that from which Henry Chadwick addressed me (then, the Olympian to the pigmy; now, the no-longer-so-young evangelical upstart to the senior, highly respected and today astonishingly persecuted teacher), I want to say to Jim: if I told you I agreed with (almost) every word you said, I hope you wouldn't conclude that you must have made some awful mistake somewhere. I am not altogether surprised at our close agreement, since I learnt so much from Jim back then and still regard myself, as he has always seen himself, as belonging in the Reformed branch of evangelical Anglicanism. Not least in that being Reformed means, among other things, a commitment to being *semper reformanda*, especially being ready to be further reformed under the Word of God. It is this that made me modify my agreement with that 'almost'. Another story will make the point.

One year in the late 1980s, I was invited to the Greenbelt Festival. Among the sessions I was to speak at, one was entitled, 'What is an Evangelical?' I wrote back to the organisers. I wasn't particularly interested in providing yet another definition of 'Evangelical'. The only possible reason for doing that, I reckoned, would be to enable people to say either, 'Phew, that's all right, I'm OK then,' or, more insidiously, 'Ah, now we know that so-and-so isn't really an Evangelical, so we can discount them,' or, worse again, 'Right: now let's reshape the church to fit this model'. In other words, people were looking, in those dangerous transitional days, for a label *which might help them to avoid having to think*. If only we could decide what an 'Evangelical' really was, we'd know that all of us really wanted to be that, and people who didn't conform were beyond our pale. The word 'Evangelical' denoted 'the thing we all want to be'. All we had to do was to clarify its contents, sigh with relief, and stop thinking.

So, in writing back to the organisers, I suggested an alternative title, in three phases. First, 'What is God calling his people to do in the coming days?' Second, 'What resources are there in the evangelical tradition to enable us to address those tasks?' And, third, 'What resources do we need for those tasks which we do *not* find in the evangelical tradition, and which we must therefore find somewhere else?' That set of questions reflects where I was then, and where I am still. I have always believed that scripture stands over all our traditions, *including our evangelical traditions*. Having sat at the feet not only of Jim Packer but of John Stott, Dick Lucas, John Wenham, Roger Beckwith and others, that was the message from them which, I believe, the Holy Spirit taught me most deeply: go deeper into scripture itself, and if that means you need to come back and tell us about things we had ignored, or got out of balance or proportion, so be it. As Jim insists in his 'Noah's Ark' study, the way then to deal with such fresh proposals is by charitable public debate, not by angry and summary rejection of anything that 'our tradition has never said before'. True Evangelicalism needs reforming from within – by the same word of God to which, characteristically, it appeals.

My own Latimer Study was, in fact – though of course I didn't realise it at the time – an advance marker for many ideas, proposals for fresh interpretations of scripture, which I have developed considerably more over the last three decades. Another memory of a telephone call comes in here, from when I was working on this Study. Roger Beckwith, then Warden of Latimer House, phoned me after reading my first draft. He said I was 'catholicizing' evangelicalism. I assumed at first that this was a rebuke: perhaps he was trying to tell me that I'd sold the pass, that Latimer shouldn't publish such a thing. Not at all. He intended it as a compliment. What's more, he helped me sharpen up some of my key points. One I remember was when, on page 112 below, I was saying that in the Old Testament the priests had a special role to the whole nation who were, collectively, a nation of priests. Nobody at the time, I said, challenged that idea. Roger suggested adding 'except Korah', which I duly and happily did. But the 'catholicizing' of which Roger spoke approvingly was not, of course, a crude attempt to include bits of Catholic theology in an evangelical framework. It was the direct result of my attempt to explore the deep roots of the New Testament in the whole story of Israel. That was what I was stumbling upon in my work both on Paul (for my doctorate) and Jesus (the beginnings of the work that led eventually to *Jesus and the Victory of God* (London: SPCK, 1996)). And I was discovering that by reconnecting with the story of Israel and the way that story came to its head in Jesus (in other words, with a way of doing biblical theology which outflanked the mere proof-texting beloved by so many) I was also reconnecting with a way of doing Christian theology which took me considerably beyond the atomistic and pragmatic ecclesiology held by many evangelicals at the time and since. As I have often put the point, if the post-reformation readings of scripture had privileged Ephesians or Colossians in the way they privileged Romans and Galatians (or rather, a particular reading of Romans and Galatians), the entire course of western theology and, in a measure, western culture and history might have been very different.

But the real problem I have with the tradition of twentieth-century English Evangelicalism I imbibed so eagerly from Jim Packer and others, and which is so elegantly set out in his summaries of evangelical belief in the two booklets printed here, is not a fine-tuning of Paul. It is the almost complete absence of the gospels. To put the matter bluntly: from the summaries of evangelical doctrine in Jim's two booklets and elsewhere, one would never know anything about Jesus except that he was divine, that he died vicariously, was raised bodily and will return in glory. So why did Matthew, Mark, Luke and John think it important – under the guidance and inspiration of the Holy Spirit – to tell us so much else? Is the story of Jesus' public career, and particularly his announcement of God's kingdom, simply a rag-bag of incidents and sayings designed to be ransacked in support of a supposedly 'Pauline' theology of 'how to get saved' and/or 'how to behave once you've been saved'? Are all those stories about what Jesus said and did simply the teaching of key doctrines and the living of a perfect life (a) to demonstrate his divinity and (b) to accomplish perfect 'righteousness' which is then imputed to us? To sharpen it up even more: how can we take seriously a statement of 'pure New Testament Christianity', claiming to honour scripture as its primary source, if it never even mentions the Kingdom of God?

Now of course some Evangelicals have, for many years, quietly construed 'kingdom of God' in terms of the Matthaean 'kingdom of heaven', and have taken the latter phrase to mean, more or less without remainder, 'heaven', as the place where God's people go when they die. Thus, 'inheriting the kingdom of heaven/God' would mean, simply and straightforwardly, 'going to heaven when you die'. Most Evangelicals have assumed, because their tradition (along with that of more or less the whole western church, Catholic and Protestant, from the high Middle Ages onwards) told them so and they weren't about to test it against sources which might have told them a very different story, that 'going to heaven when you die' was the ultimate aim and object of everything. But the Bible's own view, Jesus' own view (!), is of the kingdom of God coming 'on earth as in heaven', of the ultimate 'new heavens and new earth', and of the reign of God's people not in heaven (as in so many hymns) but on this renewed earth. From time to time this biblical viewpoint has broken back into the continuing western tradition, like a prince burgling his own palace to see what the usurpers are up to. But the western framework of thought has been too powerful, and all the returning prince has been able to achieve has been a set of proposals about eschatology, notably various millenarian theories of a coming, strange reign of God on the present earth, which the majority of western Christians, evangelical and otherwise, have regarded as frankly odd.

This is not the time or the place to go into this much further. (A fuller account is offered in my book *Surprised by Hope* (London: SPCK, 2007).) Suffice it to say (a) that Evangelicalism has always claimed to be loyal to scripture and to follow Jesus; (b) that the four gospels make it abundantly clear that Jesus explained his own public career in terms of God's kingdom coming on earth as in heaven, and that he saw his own forthcoming death as the strange means by which this would be accomplished; (c) that his first followers regarded his resurrection not as inaugurating a new way of 'going to heaven' but as the beginning of new creation, the ransoming, healing and rescue of God's good world, themselves included; (d) that these ideas, massively central to scripture, have played next to no part in traditional western, including evangelical, thought.

What would happen if they did?

For a start, they would project us swiftly forward into thinking about ways in which God's kingdom – God's sovereign, saving, Christ-shaped Spirit-driven rule on this present earth – might be worked out in practice. Shock, horror (thinks the traditional Evangelical): isn't that what those wicked liberals have been banging on about all this time? Well, yes, and some of them were indeed doing it because they had given up high Christology and cross-shaped soteriology; but some of them were doing it for the very good reason that they found it in bits of the Bible which the evangelical tradition (just like the Bultmannian tradition that Evangelicals have so denigrated!) had turned into detached nuggets that were really 'about' our own faith . . . I think, actually, that the real problem behind the sound and fury in 'conservative Evangelical' circles about the work of Steve Chalke and Brian MacLaren has not been worry over particular doctrines (though they matter, of course), but about the fact that Chalke and MacLaren think the gospel is something that has to be *done*, on the street, not merely believed. 'Isn't that,' thinks our outraged Evangelical, 'isn't that works-righteousness? Doesn't that mean getting involved in the dirty game of politics?' Well, yes, it does mean political involvement (as and when we are called to particular tasks; but it is part of the task of the church as a whole); and no, it doesn't mean works-righteousness. We work for God's kingdom, not in order to earn our salvation (though it's important to see, as in Matthew 25, a clear correlation between the works of love and mercy we do in the present and the ultimate blessedness we await by grace through faith), but because of all that Jesus was and did. As I have observed when working on the doctrine of the resurrection, it is interesting that Evangelicals began to shy away from seeing social and political action as an inherent part of the gospel – the Wilberforce vision, if you like – around the same time, and perhaps for the same reasons, as they shied away from thinking about the final bodily resurrection, and spoke instead of 'going home' to a disembodied 'heaven'.

All of this, of course, needs to be mapped on to the doctrines which classic Evangelicalism has not emphasized because it may not have thought it needed to, but which are suddenly in the middle of debate: creation and new creation. The explosion of interest in Gnosticism (as in *The Da Vinci Code*, those who haven't caught up with all this might Google 'Gospel of Thomas' and see what's going on there, or even read my little book *Judas and the Gospel of Jesus* (London: SPCK, 2006)) has been too close to Evangelicalism for comfort. As Jim Packer notes, some Evangelicals have been only a hair's breadth from dualism, from saying not only that the world lies in the power of the evil one but that the world of space, time and matter is itself evil and that the only good thing to do with it is to escape from it. Hence the classic evangelical negativity towards the arts, the sacraments, even sexuality. Hence, too, the confusions that abound when, without a road-map, Christians from an evangelical background rediscover the goodness and God-givenness of all the above but aren't sure how to express it. At this point, as elsewhere, the Reformed tradition could and should continue to teach and feed us – though I'm not sure about Jim Packer's suggestion, quoting Chesterton and Kuyper, that the only real options for thinking Christians are Catholicism and Calvinism. What about Eastern Orthodoxy, in one or more of its rich varieties? I well remember the most senior and respected English representative of Orthodoxy saying to me almost casually, in Oxford fifteen years ago, that the closest theological allies he saw around him were in the College Christian Union.

But this talk of rich varieties leads me at last to say: so where are we now, in evangelical Anglicanism and/or Anglican Evangelicalism? Has the map really become more complicated? Or is it simply that now, aged nearly 60 and with experience of living and working in many different places, I see a bit more of it than I did in 1980?

I'm sure I do now see more of what was already there, but other things have shifted dramatically as well. Let me highlight four overarching factors. No doubt much more could be said, but this is a new preface, not a new book.

To begin with, many Anglican Evangelicals are now far more conscious than they were of their *membership in a worldwide fellowship*. Ease of travel and particularly electronic communication and the internet have meant that young people (and Evangelicalism has always thrived on youthful energy) are now aware of teachers, preachers and movements from the other side of the world. A praise song written one day in Melbourne can be on a teenager's MP3 player the next day in Manchester or Mississippi. At supper the night I wrote this a composer in one of the churches in my diocese told me that she was part of an electronic network linking nearly 200,000 Christian musicians around the world. That would have been simply unthinkable even fifteen years ago, let alone thirty.

Second, the *issues* that Evangelicals face have shifted. We are no longer ranked against the classic old liberalism of Maurice Wiles and Dennis Nineham. Their reign ended quite abruptly and, though there are newer forms of liberalism, they are not (in England at least; in America all sorts of other things are happening!) straightforwardly denying basic doctrines like the Trinity, the Incarnation, the bodily resurrection, and so on. Instead, many of the theological leaders in England, people like David Ford in Cambridge, make no secret of their belief that worship, prayer and the reading of scripture are at the very centre of the whole theological enterprise. Instead, ethical 'innovation' has abounded, particularly in the area of sexual morality. Few Evangelicals thought, back in the 1970s, that we really needed to defend the orthodox line at this point. Those of us in pastoral ministry worried about how to get young people to stay chaste outside marriage, but it was assumed that we all agreed that marriage was the norm. Ethics was a special subject for those inclined to that sort of thing; many of us assumed that if we taught the Bible and good doctrine all those other things would fall into place. How wrong we were. And the reaction of many Evangelicals to the astonishing innovations, particularly in America and Canada, has shown that we desperately needed to catch up, not just with which biblical verses dealt with these issues and what they said, but with the whole area of what Oliver O'Donovan has helpfully called 'how to think about what to do'. Evangelicals have faced the challenge not only of which line to hold but of how to hold it. So far, we have only a mixed record on that front.

Third, the **unifying factors** of evangelical Anglicanism in the 1960s, which had already started to erode in the 1970s, disappeared altogether in the 1980s and 1990s. I refer, of course, to styles and modes of **public** worship. Once we knew where we were: north-end Communion (I had to explain that to an intelligent young evangelical friend the other day, when visiting a church whose hard-line evangelical vicar had the Communion table firmly against the east wall); the Book of Common Prayer with strictly limited variations; classic evangelical hymns from Wesley and others, with a fair amount of nineteenth-century pietism thrown in, all sung from a well-thumbed hymnbook (no overhead projectors) to clear and singable tunes; solid readings from scripture (either the Authorized Version or the Revised Standard) and a thorough exposition of one or both of them; open, unscripted prayer (sometimes from the congregation as well) alongside the stately Prayer Book Collects; cassock, surplice, scarf and hood; a regular 'guest service' aimed at non-Christians. Even writing out that list makes me think of old '60s movies, with Beatles-style haircuts and bright young things driving minis (or perhaps wearing them).

Much of that is gone now, swept away. The liturgical revision of the late 1970s, giving birth in England to the Alternative Service Book, accidentally gave implicit permission to many Evangelicals to do what their oaths and licences continue to tell them they shouldn't: to make up their own liturgies, to pick and choose bits and pieces and add and adapt the text on the page, or to abandon liturgy altogether. One incumbent of my acquaintance, on his first Sunday in a new parish, was putting out Communion booklets for the 8 a.m. service when the Reader rebuked him and said they didn't use books because it quenched the Spirit. I remember, as early as 1978, an undergraduate commenting to me that the College Chapel was 'high-church' because I was wearing robes at Evensong (yes, cassock, surplice, scarf and hood, just like all evangelical Anglicans in the 1960s and most in the 1970s). Now, of course, robes of any sort are regarded by some Evangelicals as dangerous or unsound, and in many places liturgy has been abandoned more or less altogether, except for a few key words at the Lord's Supper. Extraordinary practices that would have shocked 1950s evangelicals are now commonplace: for instance, someone carrying out a small table into the middle of the 'praise band' who occupy centre stage, praying a hurried prayer over the bread and wine, and then taking it away again. And many evangelicals, in charismatic and non-charismatic settings, have discovered the possibilities of different styles of prayer, such as Taizé songs. Some even light candles . . .

While on the subject of worship, two particular points stand out to me. First, the 'praise band' culture, turning worship services into overt concerts (with applause after songs), has overturned one of the cherished evangelical symbols, without, it seems, anyone much noticing. I don't just mean the frankly postmodern music, with tuneless repetitions of musical fragments; or the postmodern words which never tell much of a story but repeat bits and pieces of Christian devotion more or less at random; or the endless highlighting of a kind of romantic falling-in-love-with-Jesus spirituality which never seems to realise that romantic love is a match designed to light a more long-lasting candle. No: I mean the near-absence of the reading, or the singing, of scripture. The reading of scripture in the Anglican tradition is one of its great glories. Prayer Book (and *Common Worship*) Morning and Evening Prayer are basically showcases for scripture, which we read not simply to remind people of bits they may have forgotten but simply to declare the praises of God for his mighty acts. The clear, public reading of the Bible, Old and New Testaments, so that the congregation can hear it and understand it, is a performative celebration of what the Reformation was all about. Likewise, the Psalms are not a strange old set of poems, detached from where most people are today. They were Jesus' prayer book and they should be at the heart of ours. Woe betide a church, or a movement within a church, where the reading of scripture is a perfunctory task, a few verses stuck in before the sermon, or where the Psalms have ceased to be the heartbeat and the bloodstream of worship. One can, no doubt, keep going in this scripturally diminished mode for some while, with the energy and enthusiasm of worship carrying one forward. But such a movement needs to watch out lest it become a plant that springs up quickly but has no root. Evangelicals have always been people whose roots run deep not just into sixteenth-century traditions (which some in the newer charismatic and 'emerging' movements seem to have found less exciting than one might have hoped) but into scripture itself.

If that is my bleat of warning against the 'praise band' culture – which in other respects has a great deal going for it, especially in reaching out to young people – my second one is a warning against a movement that has concentrated so much on the Word that it is in danger of forgetting that the heart of the gospel is the Word made Flesh. One great centre of Word-based Evangelicalism recently reordered its church interior. Its bishop, telling me about it, commented, 'You know what they've done? They've turned it into a Mosque!' In other words, the church now expressed in its design a focus on the Word to the apparent exclusion of all else. Islam is a religion of the book, of the word, with its central symbol a loud voice intoning the Koran from a high pillar. The central symbol of Christianity is the cross, a vertical and a horizontal; and the most central action of the Christian faith is not the reading or preaching of the Word – though that of course must remain vital and alive as the surrounding context – but doing what Jesus told us to do when he broke the bread and poured out the wine at the Last Supper. The anti-sacramentalism of some earlier Evangelicalism (a position not shared, of course, by some of the great older evangelical heroes like the Wesleys, or the great Reformers themselves) has come to full and dangerous fruition. There are now some churches where 'doing' anything at all – processions, robes (of any kind), bowing, turning to face East, standing for the Gospel, manual acts in Communion – is frowned upon. Even kneeling, which used to be de rigueur among

Evangelicals (I remember John Stott getting out of his armchair in my study to kneel as we prepared to pray together after one conversation), is now routinely abandoned. What are we to say to all this? Simply that it embodies (ironically, since 'embodying' is what it's afraid of) a kind of theological dualism, which has passed from supposing that anything 'I do' puts me in danger of 'works-righteousness' (itself a silly idea, as the New Testament makes clear again and again) to a rejection of any activity in worship which might actually involve the body. (Of course, consciously *not* doing a particular action is just as much a 'work' as consciously doing it . . .) I have been particular shocked to hear it said, in some would-be 'reformed' Anglican circles, that the four gospels are not as important as the letters of Paul, since that is where we find 'the gospel', while the four gospels merely give us the stories of how Jesus came to die for our sins. How such a position can still claim to be 'biblical' leaves me baffled. It is, as I noted earlier, a first cousin of the theology of Rudolf Bultmann.

Fourth, there has been a development in the traditional evangelical Anglican **view of bishops**. In the 1960s and 1970s, most evangelical Anglicans didn't worry much about bishops. They were out there somewhere but they didn't interfere in parishes. When a Confirmation was required, many churches quietly used a missionary bishop on furlough (with official permission; many bishops were, and are, glad to have someone else to help with their heavy load). If the diocesan bishop had to come in person, he would, at least metaphorically, leave the car engine running while he nipped into the church, did what was required, and nipped out again. Nobody seemed to worry. Nobody imagined that you had to have a 'sound' or 'keen' bishop in order to be able to preach the gospel. In fact, from that unsatisfactory but pragmatic *modus vivendi* there grew the sense among Evangelicals that bishops were all unsound by definition, so that to become a bishop was, again by definition, to sell the pass, to compromise the gospel – but that this didn't matter in terms of what went on in the parish. It was noted that the great evangelical leaders like John Stott had refused all 'preferment', choosing instead to preach and teach the gospel – as though bishops couldn't and didn't do that (which Stott himself would never have dreamed of saying).

From time to time this attitude expressed itself in frustration that the bishops didn't discipline erring clergy. This may sometimes have been true, but often it wasn't and isn't. I remember Michael Baughen, John Stott's successor at All Souls Langham Place and then Bishop of Chester, remonstrating with such critics at a public meeting: he didn't think it was his job to give the *News of the World* a front-page story every time he swiftly and secretly dealt with someone in disgrace. But, though since Baughen there has been a steady stream of evangelicals appointed to Deaneries, Archdeaconries, senior diocesan posts and, yes, Bishoprics – naturally I declare an interest at this point – the rhetoric remains in many quarters.

But the worm has turned. Now, instead of assuming that all bishops are traitors to the cause, the same people routinely grumble, in Synods and elsewhere, (a) that they are dissatisfied with something their diocesan bishop has or hasn't said, and that they therefore threaten some kind of unilateral action to distance themselves from him, and (b) that there are no *conservative* evangelicals appointed, or not to Diocesan bishoprics. To the former complaint, one has to say, within the Church of England: yes, of course different clergy and laity will disagree with different bishops from time to time, but why should that lead you to schismatic action? It never did in the past. We are not, in England, in the same situation as some of the tragic parts of the Episcopal Church in the USA, and a few places in Canada as well, where the official teaching of the church has been changed, and where bishops now enforce radical innovations with all the legal muscle available. We are a million miles from that: we have not changed our teaching, and it's very unlikely that we shall. To the latter complaint, one is tempted to answer, You can't have it both ways: either being a bishop is a good thing, in which case you shouldn't knock those who are trying to do a difficult job with integrity; or being a bishop is a bad thing, and you shouldn't be wanting your best men (they would be men, naturally) to do it. (Oh, and who said you could call yourselves *conservative* Evangelicals? That used to mean a solid commitment to substitutionary atonement and the authority of scripture. How come those of us who still believe and teach those wonderful doctrines – who, indeed, defend them in scholarship and in the councils of the church – are denied the label?)

The real problem is, of course, that in the very flat structure of the Church of England there are, at any given moment, literally dozens of people who could easily be excellent Archdeacons; twenty or thirty who could easily be excellent Deans; and at least a dozen or two who could be first-rate diocesan bishops. Faced with that fact, and remembering that in England the Crown Nominations Commission, in which a potential candidate must gain two-thirds of the votes, consists of six representatives from the diocese and six from the national church, plus the two Archbishops, it is not surprising that the choice generally goes to someone who most people believe will be able to minister easily and effectively across the spectrum of church practice. Of course, one must maintain one's own integrity. But one must also, in the proper sense of St Paul in I Corinthians 9 (as opposed to the sneering sense often heard) make every effort to be 'all things to all people'. Not all the newly-styled 'conservatives' seem willing to embrace that Pauline vocation.

Underneath a lot of these confusions there stands the sad fact that evangelical Anglicanism has become divided, in the last generation, in a way that was almost unthinkable thirty years ago. This is reflected in the Christian Unions, where in some cases a very hard line of a particular sort has been taken, and those who disagree, who in former days would have happily continued to belong, have felt unwelcome and have set up alternative organizations. In part this has been over the divide between charismatic and non-charismatic; in part it has been over women's leadership; in part, more nebulous but quite important, it has been over a reading of the contemporary situation in terms either of the need to man the barricades against the liberal hordes or of the need to engage the contemporary culture creatively with the gospel. That either/or is itself too simplistic, but it can serve as a signpost to different *styles* rather than theologies. In fact, as I know for myself, the old ways of defining evangelicals by certain doctrines –

inspiration of scripture and substitutionary atonement, in particular – are still appealed to, but no longer really function the way they did. Sadly, party spirit and organization have taken over, with doctrines still emblazoned on the flag but other agendas, styles and aims providing the real motivation. This strange and frustrating situation, where people who have given enormous time and energy to building up Christian Unions and similar organisations in the past now find themselves blackballed for being unsound, though their beliefs have not changed, reflects a kind of Thatcherisation of English Evangelicalism, a pushy, devil-take-the-hindmost, who-cares-about-community movement which has corralled some key organisations and prevented them from truly representing the full range of evangelical opinion, declaring that it alone represents genuine Evangelicalism. Fortunately, there are many dioceses, including my own, where the evangelical clergy are far too busy with preaching and teaching the gospel to bother about such party issues, and cheerfully collaborate in mission with all those who will put their shoulder to the wheel.

We live, of course, in turbulent times. I write this on the eve of the 2008 Lambeth Conference, to which I and my colleagues go, like Paul up to Jerusalem, not knowing what awaits us there. What I do know is that the old lines of 'liberal', 'catholic' and 'evangelical', by which the Church of England used to be demarcated, have long since outlived their usefulness. As Jim Packer discovered as far back as 1968, there are times when fruitful coalitions can be formed with others who share the basic commitment to the Trinity, incarnation, atonement and resurrection – to a message and a life rooted in the real and powerful creator and redeemer God and his final saving revelation of himself in the death and resurrection of his Son, Jesus, a message and life with saving and life-transforming Spirit-given power. At a time like this it ill becomes us to draw ever tighter lines around particular positions, to dig ourselves into different ditches here and there and declare that we will die in them, and that those who will not join us in that particular ditch are obviously beyond the pale. Yes, there is much bad and dangerous theology around which we need to oppose – though the label 'liberal' itself, still waved around by some as a flag of triumph and by others as a sign of danger, is now very nearly useless except as a word which makes some people happy and others cross. There are major theological and ethical battles to be fought, and the old slogans will not help us in this urgent task. This is a time to stand up and link arms to left and right with all who will work for the renewal of the church in mission, holiness and unity, including taking the uncomfortable decisions that are going to be necessary for that to come about. Evangelicals have made enormous contributions to the life and health of the Church of England and the wider Anglican Communion in many generations past. It would be tragic if, after all the great gains of the last generation or two, we were to squander it all in factional in-fighting.

Above all, we need to pray. Evangelical Anglican Identity, rethought once more around the Bible, the Gospel and the Church, always was rooted in prayer, and always should be. God is God; Jesus is Lord; the Spirit is powerful and unpredictable; the only identity that really matters is that of the humble Christian, holding the world and the church before God in earnest and fervent prayer, and ready then to work when, where, how and with whom God directs. May God help us in these times not to think 'I am of Paul', or 'I am of Apollos', but 'I am of Christ'. And perhaps, as we do so, to discover unexpected friends, and not to think, as we work alongside them, that we must have made some terrible mistake somewhere.

N.T. WRIGHT

JULY 2008

THE EVANGELICAL ANGLICAN IDENTITY PROBLEM: AN ANALYSIS

BY J. I. PACKER

first published 1978

Latimer Study 1 Contents

1.   A Difficulty of Definition

Let me begin with some brooding. Am I an evangelical? Certainly, since the days when as an undergraduate I was converted and nurtured in a University Christian Union, and introduced to a lively Anglican evangelical church in the process, I have thought I was. When I learned of the evangelical tradition in history, as seen in men like Augustine; the Reformers; the Puritans; Edwards, Whitefield and Wesley; Ryle, Spurgeon, Finney, Moody and Hudson Taylor in the last century, and more recently B. B. Warfield and C. T. Studd, I believed myself to identify with all the main things they had stood for, and accordingly lined myself up with the Inter-Varsity Fellowship of Evangelical Unions (now the Universities' and Colleges' Christian Fellowship) and the 'definite' evangelicals in the Church of England. A curacy in a black-gown church, and two decades of organizing the annual Puritan and Reformed Studies Conference at Westminster Chapel, served only to strengthen this commitment. In 1958, in *'Fundamentalism' and the Word of God* I argued that 'evangelicals' was the proper name for those whose critics were calling them 'fundamentalists', and as one of those to whom James Barr in his recent trying book *Fundamentalism* applies the old label I say the same today. To me, the 'vibes' of the word 'evangelical' are wholly good and its meaning is wholly positive; I think it is an honour to a man to be so called, and I would not wish ever to be described or referred to in any other way.

But in the seventies individual evangelicals both orally and in print have questioned my right to bear the name, for the following reasons (as I understand them).

First, in 1970 I was one of two evangelicals who wrote a book called *Growing into Union* along with two 'catholic' spokesmen, Professor E. L. Mascall and the present Bishop of Truro (then of Willesden). Though we all could and did endorse all that the book said, we were acting on the principle which Francis Schaeffer calls 'co-belligerence' – that is, we made common cause on particular issues without committing ourselves to agree beyond

27

that point. Schaeffer rightly distinguishes co-belligerence from compromise, but some saw this venture of cooperation as intrinsically compromising, and at least one journal later told the world that in virtue of it I could not be regarded as an evangelical any longer.

Second, *Growing into Union* urged that the historic episcopate in its developed form, though not necessary to the church's existence or to the adequacy of its spiritual experience and pastoral care in any particular case, has positive value as a sign of Christ's continuing ministry to his people, and therefore of the church's own unity, continuity and continuing identity by reason of Christ's ministry; so it ought to be retained by the Church of England, and commended in these terms to non-episcopal churches. That was and is my opinion. Most Anglican evangelicals, however, have hitherto approved diocesan episcopacy, insofar as they have approved it at all, merely on pragmatic grounds, as an institution of proved pastoral worth, and they have declined to see any distinctive theological significance in it. Though I have been privileged to watch a number of bishops ministering superbly, as good stewards of their episcopal prerogatives, I confess I should find it hard to vindicate this pragmatic warrant for episcopacy against the pragmatic counter-argument in the Dissentient View appended to the 1959 Anglican-Methodist report, and in the late Ian Henderson's *Power without Glory*: namely, that on balance, taking a broad view of its record over more than a millennium and a half, the historic episcopate appears as so tainted an institution that it is not worth trying to re-claim; and to ask non-episcopal churches to accept it as a price they must pay for union or even full communion with the Church of England is an offensive impertinence. The argument that existing episcopacy should be reformed and retained, rather than abolished and replaced, because of its long-standing significance as a sign of something important, seems to me not only sound in itself but also the only viable answer to this contention. But I have been told that my doctrine of episcopacy is 'higher' than Anglican evangelicals hold, so that my continued right to call myself an evangelical is doubtful.

Third, the declaration of the gospel in *Growing into Union*, despite our strong stress on justification by faith, was criticized by some (not, I think, Anglicans) as unevangelical because sacramentalist. The point here, however, seemed to be that the critics held a pseudo-Zwinglian 'bare sign', as opposed to 'efficacious sign', view of baptism and the Lord's supper, and thought that all other evangelicals did too, and had not reckoned with the fact that the Anglican confessional position, like that set forth in Calvin's *Institutes*, is less negative than this. I think it is clear from the *Institutes* that Calvin would not have found fault with *Growing into Union* at this point. (But then, was he an evangelical? Some hold views which imply that he was only half-way to being one.)

Fourth, I was a member of the now-defunct Doctrine Commission which produced the report *Christian Believing*, an exercise in interpretative description (phenomenology) rather than in normative thinking. This report, which has the character of a graceful guide to a confused noise, was a bitter disappointment to many, including some of its authors; but it was all that a body more or less equally divided between 'rads' and 'trads' could produce, and as information about what different folk do and do not believe and why, it has its own modest use. I have been told, however, that no signatory of the report can be regarded any more as an evangelical, since critical normative theology is all that an evangelical will ever allow himself to engage in, and *Christian Believing* is certainly not that. All reviews of the report which I saw in evangelical journals treated it as if it ought to be normative, and were therefore more or less hostile, as was natural. One of these mistaken reviews censured me by name, and when I wrote to set the record straight the editor would not print my letter.

Fifth, it has been said by some in recent years that evangelicals believe in the inerrancy of Scripture, and on this basis reject as contrary to Scripture all forms of the theory of evolution. I believe in the inerrancy of Scripture, and maintain it in print, but exegetically I cannot see that anything Scripture says, in the first chapters of Genesis or anywhere else, bears on the biological theory of evolution one way or the other. On that theory itself, as a non-scientist, watching from a distance the disputes of the experts, I suspend judgment, but I recall that B. B. Warfield was a theistic evolutionist. If on this account I am not an evangelical, then neither was he.

Sixth, it is also claimed, against me among others, that no Anglican, not even a Bible-believing five-point Calvinist who cares for evangelism like myself, can be called an evangelical without qualification, since evangelical principles require that church membership be limited to those who credibly profess orthodox evangelical faith, whereas the Church of England is doctrinally mixed and embraces many who could not identify themselves as evangelicals in this way. This is tantamount to claiming that all true evangelicals are committed to Baptist or Congregationalist church principles, as these were universally held from the seventeenth century to the nineteenth, which seems a bold thing to say; but one still hears it said.

The purpose of these reminiscences is to make the point that anyone who proposes to define the word 'evangelical' must go carefully. Sectarian influences, counselling various forms of exclusiveness, and shibboleths deriving from partisan memories, sometimes remote, can creep in on the one hand to narrow the definition unduly; on the other hand, desire to claim the word, with all its good vibrations, can produce definitions of undue vagueness ('low church', 'emphasizing personal experience', etc.); and honest differences of opinion as to what evangelical faith allows and rules out on secondary matters are doubtless inescapable in any case. And if one attempts a strictly historical definition there are still pitfalls. 'Evangelical' as a term of identification was first used by Lutherans in Reformation days. By the nineteenth century it was being applied generally to any people or activities, both Anglican and nonconformist, that stood in line with the eighteenth century awakening and its offshoots, the movement which by then was being called the Evangelical Revival. The word 'evangelicalism' was coined at that time to signify the style of Christianity which evangelicals embraced, with its doctrine, experience and practical priorities – that is, its theology, spirituality and policy. For a century and more it has been understood that to be an evangelical is to identify with all three. But evangelical theology, spirituality and policy have never been quite homogeneous. This is because two distinguishable streams of tradition have flowed together to create the evangelical identity, without ever perfectly merging, and different evangelicals both in and outside the Church of England stand in one stream rather than the other. One is the confessional, churchly, anti-Roman Catholic Protestantism of the sixteenth century, with its passion for revealed truth and its strong intellectual, theological and cultural drive. The other is the pietism which emerged within Protestant state churches in the seventeenth and eighteenth centuries, pacific and intellectually unenterprising, but with a passion for vital spiritual experience. Pietism reacted against spiritual deadness and stressed personal faith, rebirth, soul-culture and informal fellowship. The 'keen' group (*ecclesiola in ecclesia*), the little church within the church, or a Society of Moravian or Methodist type, or an informal gathering in a home for prayer or Bible searching or sharing experience) was its main structure, and evangelism in one form or another was its prime concern. Pietism, no less than national Protestantism, saw itself as the true heir of the Reformation, and evangelicalism has developed as a blend of the two streams; but individuals, groups and churches vary considerably as to where in the total flow they stand.

Yet these differences must not be overstressed. On fundamentals all evangelicals are at one. Thus, all evangelicalism is based on the doctrines of the Trinity; Christ's deity; the correlation of grace and faith; justification by faith through Christ's substitutionary atonement; Christ's physical resurrection and present reign; new birth and progressive sanctification through the ministry of the indwelling Spirit; the church as the fellowship of all believers; and the certainty of Christ's personal return. Also, all evangelicalism rests, from a formal and methodological standpoint, on the final authority of Holy Scripture – for (says Loraine Boettner in *Baker's Dictionary of Theology*, p. 200) 'when this tenet is granted the other doctrines of the evangelical faith follow as a matter of course.' Also, all evangelicalism sees evangelism as a constant priority for the church, and maintains a Christ-centred spirituality in which fellowship with the risen Lord by faith is central. Such differences as evangelicals have on doctrine (e.g., Calvinism and Arminianism; covenant theology and dispensationalism; pre-, post- and non-millenialism; paedobaptism and believer's baptism), and on experience (e.g., whether the 'second blessing' in its Wesleyan, Keswick or Pentecostal form is a norm; whether 'charismatic' experience, e.g., glossolalic prayer and prophecy, should be sought or not), and on practice (e.g., methods of evangelism, and ways of socio-cultural community involvement) are secondary and, so to speak, within the family. So are the noticeable differences between congregations in the rate at which, and the extent to which, they respond to cultural change and the shifting preoccupations of folk around them. These differences may cause strain on the surface, but evangelical unity is a reality wherever these biblical principles of faith and life are truly acknowledged. It is in terms of these principles that evangelicalism ought to be defined.

2. Attitudes to Doctrine and the Church

Before offering a definition, however, it will be worth while to reflect briefly on two questions, both of which arise naturally from what has been said and bear directly on today's situation. The first is, why English evangelicals should be so ready to censure each other and divide from each other when differences of theological opinion emerge. Is it mere natural cantankerousness, or what? The second question is, why Anglican evangelicals should have an identity problem at all at the present time. Are they under some kind of inner strain, or is there an external reason?

2.1. A conscience about truth

To the first question, the answer is that the sensitive reactions of English evangelicals to apparent shifts from orthodoxy within their own ranks expresses something basic to the evangelical mentality – namely, the sense of being entrusted with revealed truth, and of having a steward's responsibility to keep the deposit intact. Evangelicalism everywhere is the religion of a biblically-informed conscience. Private judgment, as evangelicals inculcate it, has to do not with the layman's luxury of disagreeing with the organised church, but with the universal necessity of agreeing with the Bible, and therefore with the universal duty of doing as the Bereans did and searching the Scriptures to see whether what men say in God's name is really so (Acts 17:11). One thing which Scripture emphasizes is the Christian's responsibility to hold fast and profess consistently the teaching God has given, whatever inducements and pressures there may be to let it go. Paul, John and the writer to the Hebrews highlight this responsibility, both by teaching it directly and by risking the personal odium of actively challenging particular doctrinal errors. The tolerant indifferentism which reflects belief that there are no revealed truths and no given certainties, so that no finality can attach to any biblical or post-biblical formulations, and therefore Christianity must be viewed as essentially a life rather than a doctrine, is as far as possible from the evangelical outlook. The authentic evangelical mind is angularly dogmatic, just because the archetypal Christian instruction given in the New Testament is itself so. In his book *The Christian Mind*, Harry Blamires, an Anglican catholic, argues that the marks of a Christian mind are six: its supernatural orientation, its awareness of evil, its conception of truth as objective and absolute, its acceptance of authority, its concern for persons and the personal dimensions of life, and its sacramental cast, seeing earth's aspirations and joys as pointers to God and heaven. Evangelicals agree, and recognise that such a mind is essentially dogmatic in the double sense of both receiving and affirming Christian dogma. Christians are stewards of truth, and must fulfil their ministry by upholding it in face of error that would destroy it or vagueness and compromise that would blue it. This, as evangelicals view the matter, is an integral part of the service which Christians must render to their Lord.

So when brother evangelicals dismissed me from the particular involvements I had with them, thinking I had betrayed the faith of the gospel, and when Francis Schaeffer at Lausanne (1974) and Harold Lindsell in *Battle for the Bible* (1976) blew the whistle on the diminished view of Holy Scripture with which some American evangelicals appeared to have taken up, though the gestures were disruptive and their appropriateness could be questioned, they were authentic expressions of an active evangelical conscience, with its consuming, God-taught passion not to lose any God-given truth. They were gestures to respect, therefore, even if one should conclude they were mistaken.

This century has seen wide use in both the Church of England and the larger Protestant churches of the U.S.A. of the distinction between 'liberal' and 'conservative' evangelicalism. This distinction, which 'conservative' evangelicals did not draw and which, as usually expounded, seems to them inaccurate (for anyone who inclines to what is usually called 'liberal' theology is to that extent not an evangelical at all), seems originally to have been meant to express the Gilbertian view that in Christianity, as in politics, the basic differences are less of conviction than of temperament and habit of mind, since 'every child that's born into this world alive is either a little Liberal or else a little Conservative'. Certainly, the 'conservative' evangelical is regularly stereotyped as one whose roots are in the past, not the present, and whose thinking looks back theologically to 'the good old days' of the Reformers, Puritans and their eighteenth and nineteenth century successors, while the 'liberal' evangelical, not carrying the same weight of traditional intellectual luggage, is seen as free, in a way that his opposite number is not, to adjust to current movements of thought and to recast his theology into new forms. In any case, according to stereotype, the liberal's basic loyalty is to the figure of Jesus Christ rather than to any particular dogmatic assertions that the Bible makes about him. The implication is that the same would be true for the 'conservative' also, were it not that his backward-looking timidity or conventionality of mind keeps him from seeing this point. During the past half-century able, warm-hearted, vigorous 'liberal' evangelicals have given much to the world church. Yet in holding to a hermeneutic which sees man's witness to God in Holy Scripture as in the last analysis a little less than God's own witness to himself, 'liberals' fall short of the authentic evangelical conscience and sense of responsibility regarding revealed doctrine. Those called 'conservatives' (who prefer to call themselves evangelicals with no qualifying adjective) go beyond the 'liberals' in urging that loyalty to Christ entails accepting the Bible from his hand, as it were, as the infallible guidance of Father, Son and Spirit for Christian belief and behaviour, and holding through thick and thin to everything that it sets forth. The difference that this makes is considerable.

Here, however, evangelicals need to be self-critical, for the authentic evangelical concern for revealed truth can itself be corrupted by motivations much murkier than a pure desire to see the church faithful to God and fruitful among men.

Thus, fear of being scoffed at or swamped, and the defensiveness that is born of the memory of past roastings for our views, can work in us an obstinate, blinkered, suspicious and rigid immobility ('our doctrine, right or wrong; and if Scripture said that Jonah swallowed the whale I'd believe it!'): and this attitude falls far short of being a responsible stewardship of truth. The White Queen may have learned to believe six impossible things before breakfast, but that is not an art which Christians are required to master, for we do not honour God by believing absurdities. Again, 'domino' theories charting the expected course of apostasy ('let this point go, and all Christianity will fall') spring naturally from the fear-ridden mind. Without for a moment suggesting that such Cassandra-cries are never justified, it has to be said that their intensity is not always the measure of their realism, nor is scaremongering always a sign of deep spirituality.

Pride, too, can betray here. Christians learn from Scripture to understand their calling in remnant terms – that is, to recognize that the church, which was itself originally the authentic remnant of genealogical Israel, may, like Israel after the flesh, lapse in part, so that at any time on major issues of godliness the Christian may find himself in relative isolation, or standing with only a few, like the faithful few of Sardis (Revelation 3:4). Discipleship to the once-isolated Christ requires of us readiness for this. But there is a carnal counterpart to remnant thinking, and that is sectarian pride, which much too cheerfully accepts and even courts isolation, waiving the attempt to (in Jude's words) 'convince some, who doubt; save some, by snatching them out of the fire' (Jude 22f.).

Such withdrawal into the backwaters and backwoods of obscurity may look heroic to the casual gaze, but, like other forms of censorious stand-offishness, it may have at its heart nothing more respectable than the exclusiveness of C. S. Lewis' 'inner ring' – the fewer we are together, the merrier we shall be. Furthermore, the siege mentality that comes of being, and feeling, threatened can produce an unhealthy passion for uniformity among those who are seen as defenders of truth's beleaguered citadel, and a ruthless readiness to brand as traitors any who are thought to have stepped out of line. Obscurely but potently the feeling emerges that external pressures forbid indulgence of any kind of eccentricity, and that those who do not see this are for that very reason a danger best destroyed.

Again, loyalty to 'the standard of teaching to which you were committed' (Romans 6:17) is a duty and a virtue, but it can easily be corrupted into a rationalistic self-sufficiency which will not allow that there is anything to be learned from Scripture which evangelicals do not already know, or that any biblical truth could be made clearer by expressing it in different words from those which evangelicals now use. Any who lapse into this intellectual perfectionism will be sharp, no doubt, against their brothers who go into dialogue about divine things in hope that new insights into the meaning of Scripture will come to them from their non-evangelical partners.

Yet intellectual self-sufficiency must be judged a delusion that damages (because it limits) those who embrace it, and it is worth a great deal of self-scrutiny to ensure that neither you nor I become its victim.

With these caveats, however, the evangelical principle of venerating (not worshipping, but revering) the Bible as source, medium and touchstone of revealed truth, and of challenging and censuring views, even when held by professed evangelicals, that seem not to do justice to the Bible, ought to be vindicated and sustained; and if the impression left is of an unlovely quarrelsomeness, it must be urged that sensitiveness about doctrine is fundamentally a healthy thing, and it is better that misjudgments be made out of zeal for truth than that men should be able to live in peace because that zeal is lacking.

2.2. *A commitment to the Church*

To the second question, why Anglican evangelicals should have an identity problem at this time, the answer is that the past generation has seen more change in the Church of England than at any time since the Reformation, and this, plus the new patterns of cooperation whereby resurgent Anglican evangelicalism has shared in making the alterations, has left in the minds of both Anglican and non-Anglican evangelicals a fear that the accumulation of particular changes, and the throwing of so many established procedures into the melting-pot, may have affected the character of Anglican evangelicalism more than Anglican evangelicals themselves are aware. So there is a good deal of sharp questioning from evangelicals outside the Church of England, and a good deal of heart-searching among those within it.

To be more specific. Since the middle of the century the Church of England has adopted new canons, a new formula of clerical subscription, and new alternative services, differing in both content and style from those of 1662. It has introduced synodical government. It has centralized finance and reorganized the parishes by amalgamation of parishes and closure of churches to an unprecedented degree. It has talked unity (which is not identical with union, though some never draw the distinction) both with the main Free Churches and in a preliminary way with Roman Catholics. It has diversified ministry by introducing clerical groups and teams, by establishing a supporting, non-stipendiary class of presbyters, and by smiling on experiments with pastoral and leadership groups of laymen working with incumbents. In the middle of all this, at the Keele Congress of 1967 a representative thousand evangelicals, half clergy and half laity, conscious of their new vitality, leadership and academic strength, committed themselves henceforth to accept the Church's problems and concerns as their own and to contribute as positively as they could in every part of the Church's ongoing life. This pledge of new involvement closed a generation-long chapter of evangelical detachment. Most Anglican evangelicals since 1967 have moved the Keele way, and the Nottingham Congress of 1977 shows them at least trying still to do so.

What Keele meant for evangelicals was spelt out in advance by Peter Johnston in his chairman's address to the Islington Conference some weeks before the Congress met. 'The Church of England is changing ... Evangelicals in the Church of England are changing too. Not in doctrinal conviction (for the truth of the gospel cannot change) but (like any healthy child) in stature and posture. It is a tragic thing ... that Evangelicals have a very poor image in the Church as a whole. We have acquired a reputation for narrow partisanship and obstructionism ... We need to repent and to change ... I for one desire to be rid of all sinful "party spirit". *Evangelical* is not a party word ...' What Peter Johnston desired, and Keele pledged, has largely become fact; evangelicals today are more deeply involved in the inner life of the Church of England than ever before, and the old days of entrenched 'party' isolationism are gone.

But, as we said, this change has raised questions. The old pre-war ethos of parochial aloofness – established independency, maintained by the parson's freehold and trust patronage, with minimal diocesan links – is no more. The old symbols of evangelical identity – north side; no stole or candles; exclusive use of 1662 worship forms; the eschewing of tobacco, alcohol and the cinema; deep dog-collars; etc. – are now mostly things of the past. The language of Zion, that spiritual Swahili made up from the Authorized Version and the old hymns, which Anglican and non-Anglican evangelicals once spoke in just about the same way, has given place to several distinct dialects, based apparently on different modern versions of Scripture and agreeing only in addressing God as 'you' rather than 'thou'. Pressure of time on evangelical clergy and laity as they work out their deepened commitment to the Church of England means that they now have much more to do with other Anglicans than with non-Anglican evangelicals. The Church of England currently makes gestures towards the Roman Catholic Church that are more friendly and forthcoming than ever before, yet evangelicals seem not to worry as their fathers would have worried. The rumbling hiccups and fumbling pickups on doctrinal points which were sometimes noticeable at Nottingham confirmed suspicions that, whatever else evangelical clergy had been doing since Keele, they had not been spending their strength drilling folk in basic evangelical principles as their fathers used to do.

What does all this add up to? What does it mean? What does it show? Are Anglican evangelicals what they were? Anglican evangelicals say they are changing as truth and the times together require, but non-Anglican evangelicals, many of whom retain almost all the outward style of their own spiritual fathers and grandfathers, tend to urge that the changes which Anglicans currently accept mark a radical erosion of their evangelicalism, so that soon it will be a mere featureless blob, like the ruined, unrecognisable face of a weatherbeaten gargoyle. Also, they urge, it is already clear that from being Anglican evangelicals, men who found their deepest identity in their evangelical faith as such, they have now become evangelical Anglicans, finding their deepest identity in their denomination as such, and this surely is defection. Some Anglicans, hearing this, are unimpressed, but others are troubled. They are anxious that the accusation should be false, but fear that it may be a truer bill than they or their leaders realise. Could it be that the non-Anglican spectators are seeing most of the Church of England game?

The Anglican evangelical identity problem is rooted in these facts and fears. What is in question is where Anglican evangelicals think they are going, what they are taking with them of their former convictions, and what policies their present outlook may suggest or allow; and whether, in the light of the answer to these three enquiries, it is proper to go on calling them evangelicals at all. My present purpose is to speak to this question, or complex of questions, and to do so in a prescriptive and persuasive way rather than just descriptively - that is, I want to spell out ideals, and urge what I think should be, rather than limit myself to chronicling what is. After all, since evangelicals, like other Christians, are at best imperfectly sanctified sinners, actual evangelicalism, whether

Anglican or non-Anglican, like every other Christian movement, will always appear as an imperfect product which at its best is leaving what is behind to press on to what lies ahead, prayerfully resolved by God's grace to do better tomorrow than yesterday. So one renders truer service to evangelicalism by trying to refocus its goals and standards in the light of grace than by personating the law in criticism of its present state. That is the service I shall try to render now.

As a first step, I offer an account of essential evangelicalism which will, I hope, commend itself as a true and adequate frame of reference for the rest of the discussion.

3.   The Anatomy of Evangelicalism

The following paragraphs sketch out evangelicalism in the ideal terms in which evangelicals themselves see it.   How far in practice any of us realise this ideal, whether in our church or inter-denominational groupings or in our personal lives, is a separate question, on which I do not attempt to pronounce.   But, whether we manage to be good evangelicals or only bad ones, the ideal seems fairly clear, and fairly well agreed wherever groups taking to themselves the evangelical name are found.   My analysis involves four general claims which focus the evangelical self-understanding and six particular beliefs which, though each belonging (as evangelicals think) to mainstream Christianity, and thus as far from eccentricity as possible, add up together to a position that is quite distinctive in the world church.

3.1.   Evangelical claims

Practical Christianity

The first claim is that evangelicalism is **practical** Christianity, a matter of total discipleship whereby human beings with all their powers become wholly subject to the Lord Jesus Christ, the divine-human mediator, in all the glory of his person, place and saving work.   In other words, evangelicalism is not just a theology, or a spirituality, or a plan of action, but is all these three blended together in a 'principled' life-style which embraces relationships with God, with men and with ourselves both in private and in public, at home, at work, in church and across the board in society.

The strong personal disciplines and restraints of the evangelical life-style have sometimes made it appear as a kind of monasticism outside the cloister, and certainly forsaking the world in the sense of renouncing 'worldliness', that is, the world's way, and consenting to swim culturally against the stream, is a theme which has always had prominence in evangelical devotional teaching.

> Take up thy cross, the Saviour said,
> If thou wouldst my disciple be:
> Deny thyself, the world forsake,
> And humbly follow after me

– these words of C.W. Everest, often on evangelical lips, express an insight into the meaning of Christianity which is basic to the evangelical outlook. Evangelicals are clear that without commitment to the living Christ against the world, with readiness for conflict anywhere and everywhere, you cannot be an evangelical, for you cannot be a Christian at all. Yet it must be stressed that in their opposition to the world evangelicals, following Scripture (cf. 1 John 2:15f.), are opposing not what is natural, but what is sinful. Evangelicals may pitch their tents within a hair's breadth of Manicheism (after all, Manicheism really does couch at the door for all who have noticed that the New Testament rates this era evil, cf. Galatians 1:3), but, like the prospector's hut in Chaplin's *The Gold Rush*, evangelicalism never quite falls into the abyss on whose edge it teeters. There are no areas of created life whose goodness it does not affirm, or which it dismisses as unredeemable, just as there are no created joys, intellectual or sensuous, which it hesitates to sanctify. Though the pietistic streak in the make-up of evangelicalism has sometimes led to narrow and negative thinking about the social and cultural implications of biblical faith, a breadth of positive concern for what life in this rich and varied world can become by grace, and a sense of responsible

Christian stewardship in social and cultural matters, is more deep-rooted in the tradition, and has been so since Calvin's day at least.

Pure Christianity

The second claim is that evangelicalism is *pure* Christianity. This claim, be it said, is voiced not as a conceited boast, but as a humble confession made in gratitude by Christians who see the value of what they have received. Purity, doctrinal, ecclesiastical and ethical, was a major concern of the Reformers and Puritans, and evangelicals today think of reformation and revival in terms of restoring pure Christianity. They claim that in principle, if not always (alas) in practice, evangelicalism is pure Christianity as such, free from accretions and dilutions. The claim is admittedly bold, but, as they think, necessary, because true.

So when Anglican evangelicals 'make their contribution', as the saying is, to the larger Anglican mix, they do so in the belief that hereby they are privileged to call the whole Church into paths of faithful obedience and spiritual renewal. And when evangelicals of any denomination are invited to see their theology as one strand or fragment of truth needing to be set in a larger ecumenical framework they demur, humbly but firmly insisting that, on the contrary, evangelical theology itself provides the framework into which all biblical insights should be fitted, and that any deviating from this framework will be to that extent a deviating from Christianity. Evangelicals see all theological truth as belonging by right to evangelical theology, and evangelical theology as belonging by right to the whole Christian church.

But what are the criteria of 'pure' Christianity? All evangelicals would, I think, answer this question first by identifying pure Christianity as the consistent living out of pure Christian beliefs, and second by appealing to Paul's negative and positive criteria of pure belief. The negative criterion is, no intrusion of human wisdom or works into our understanding of God's salvation, but total openness to, and dependence on, what God reveals to us in his Word and what he does for us in his grace (see 1 Corinthians 1-2; Colossians 1-3; Galatians 3-5; Romans). The positive criterion is that the dignity and role of Christ the mediator who in his threefold office as prophet, priest and king is our wisdom, righteousness, sanctification, redemption, peace, life and hope in person (see 1 Corinthians 1:30; Ephesians 2:14; Colossians 3:4; 1 Timothy 1:1), should be adequately acknowledged. In thus seeking to avoid both extraneous matter which would distort the good news and shoddy formulations which would tarnish or trivialize it, evangelicalism understands itself as 'mere Christianity', and will, with Paul, enter into strenuous polemics to maintain its point of view.

Thus, in the sixteenth-century Reformation conflict its concerns came to be crystallized in five motto phrases each containing the word *only* (Latin, *solus*) – *sola Scriptura*, *solo Christo*, *sola fide*, *sola gratia*, *soli Deo gloria* (by Scripture only; by Christ only; by faith only; by grace only; glory to God only). The thoughts which these slogans expressed were that we know God through Scripture alone, by attending to what is written and eschewing speculations which in claiming to supplement biblical teaching would actually relativize it; that we are saved through Christ's mediation and his blood shed for us, and have no other source of hope; that we are justified through faith in Christ alone apart from our works; that we are saved, first to last, by God's loving initiative and power alone, not by our own endeavour; and that praise for our salvation must be given to God alone, none of the credit being due to us. Given the framework of Trinitarian belief and the awareness that the created order is the theatre of God's redemptive action, the renewing of creation being redemption's goal, these five beliefs are still the backbone of pure Christianity as evangelicals understand it.

Before moving on, we should notice that with the claim to purity goes a claim to finality, based on the insight that you cannot add to Christian faith, thus understood, without subtracting from it. By augmenting it, you necessarily impoverish it. Should you, for example, add to it a doctrine of human priestly mediation, or of angelic mediation, as the Colossians did, you would obscure the perfect adequacy of the mediatorial ministry which Christ fulfils. Should you add a doctrine of human merit alongside Christ's merit, as in effect the Galatians did, you would effectively deny the perfect adequacy of Christ's righteousness and blood-shedding as the ground of our pardon and acceptance. Should you add the thought that the essence of Holy Communion is in some sense, symbolic or real, the sacrificing of Christ and of ourselves in him, you would crowd out the knowledge that the central action in Holy Communion is receiving Christ and his benefits through faith in the 'visible word' of the sacramental sign. The principle applies across the board; at every point in our relationship with God, evangelical theology sets 'Christ *only*' in opposition to all forms of religious self-assertion, whether theological, ecclesiastical or devotional. What is more than evangelical is thus less than evangelical. Evangelical belief, by its very nature, cannot be supplemented, only denied. The insights of other theologies can be set in an evangelical framework without loss, and to their own great advantage, but the basic convictions of evangelical theology cannot be set in another framework without their meaning being so changed as to be effectively lost.

Unitive Christianity

The third claim made is that evangelicalism is *unitive* Christianity. Sometimes evangelicals are thought to be sectarian in spirit, or weak in their view of the church, because for over a century their interdenominational fellowship structures, local and worldwide, have seemed to command more of their love and loyalty than do their own denominations. But this is a mistake. The evangelical will certainly say that his prime commitment is to the worldwide evangelical brotherhood as such, and that he is closer to evangelicals outside his own denominational family than he can be to members of his own church who deny or query basics of his faith. What this reflects, however, is not schismatic individualism or sectarian instincts, but the evangelical ecumenical vision: for what evangelicals have desired ever since the conflicts of the sixteenth century is reformation and renewal throughout the world church on the basis and by the means of evangelical theology.

Evangelicals since Calvin and Cranmer have longed to see

world Christian unity; meaning by unity agreement in the faith, plus mutual love, plus a welcome at the Lord's Table to all believers in good standing in any part of the church, plus cooperation in maintaining and spreading the gospel. But evangelicals today, facing the confused half-belief which at present pervades most of the older and larger Protestant churches, find it necessary to insist on some things which their Reformation forebears could take for granted – namely, that it is gospel truth, rather than formal denominational links, that must fix the bounds of fellowship and determine just how much Christian closeness can be realised, and how much cooperation practised, in any given situation. Evangelicals see fellowship in the gospel – confessional fellowship, whereby we celebrate each other's faithful stewardship of God's truth – as the first form of ecumenism, out of which every other element grows; and they hope for a day when the worldwide church, taught and moved by the Spirit of God himself, will come to share this fellowship. Their attitude follows directly from their valuation of the faith which they received, as they believe, from God. From within the World Council of Churches one sometimes hears it said that the church must let the world write its agenda for mission, but the World Council itself claims the prerogative of writing the church's agenda for ecumenism, and because evangelicals quarrel with items on that agenda they are constantly stereotyped as anti-ecumenical. The truth is, however, that evangelicals quarrel with the W.C.C. agenda because they have a different ecumenical vision – one to which unity in evangelical faith is fundamental.

To live consistently in terms of this vision is not easy, as evangelical Anglicans in particular keep finding. Consistency prompts them to call themselves Anglican evangelicals rather than evangelical Anglicans, to show that it is the gospel as such, rather than the Anglican heritage as such, which determines their Christian identity and directs their practice of Christian fellowship. (In fact, they see a massive overlap between the gospel and the Anglican heritage, which is why they remain Anglicans, even enthusiastic Anglicans, despite all their discontents with Anglicanism at present; but the biblical gospel and the Anglican tradition are at least formally distinct.) Fellow-Anglicans, however, sometimes interpret their attitude as showing looseness of Anglican allegiance. Consistency also requires them to pursue a bilateral policy of cooperative association with evangelicals in other denominations, alongside constructive reforming involvement in their own; and Free Church evangelicals sometimes construe this bilateralism as a sign that their Anglican brethren wish they were out of the Church of England but lack the guts to leave. Some Free Church evangelicals go on to argue that by staying in the same denominational framework as this or that unorthodox clergyman Anglican evangelicals become guilty of his heresies – guilty, not by personal affirmation, but by association and acquiescence. However unjustifiable in itself, this guilt-by-association argument may do good under God by rousing Anglican evangelicals to yet more vigorous debate against mis-belief, but it is for all that hard to bear.

Yet the vision remains valid. The evangelical goal of unity in faith is in principle practical politics. Evangelicals appeal, and teach others to appeal, to Holy Scripture as God's standard, and they employ an analogy-of-Scripture hermeneutic which assumes the coherence of the biblical message and lets one passage illuminate another. On this basis genuine agreement on matters of faith is possible. Indeed, it is actual; the stability over four and a half centuries of international evangelical belief on all essentials of the faith {including the important tenet that no particular church order is an essential of the faith) is so remarkable that it goes far to confirm the claim that here in truth is the doctrinal core of Christianity. By contrast, Christians who do not follow this method of determining beliefs, but rely instead on Christian tradition criticized more or less radically by Christian reason, are unlikely ever to reach stable agreement among themselves.

Rational Christianity

The fourth claim is that evangelicalism is **rational** Christianity. This needs highlighting, for the pietistic and charismatic preoccupation with experience, and the grotesque rationalistic

46

obscurantism of some 'fundamentalist' writing on God and his ways (mainly American, but it sells in England), tend to obscure the intellectual strength of evangelicalism as we meet it in, say, John Calvin, John Owen, Jonathan Edwards, James Orr and B. B. Warfield. But to stress the reasonableness, coherence and explanatory power of evangelical belief, and to encourage competent apologetics, has in truth been the common evangelical way; anti-intellectualism is a defensive development, recent and uncharacteristic, a result of feeling swamped by prejudice, hurt by ridicule and outgunned in technical learning. It was marked among British evangelicals in all the churches between the two wars, but is vanishing as evangelical competence and nerve are regained.

These four claims set the perspective from which the six convictions that follow should be viewed.

3.2. Evangelical fundamentals

These convictions are:

The supremacy of Holy Scripture

Evangelicals explain the canonical status of the 66 biblical books in terms of their being both sufficient and self-interpreting (theologically, that is) as a guide from God on all matters of faith and practice. Evangelicals call the Bible the Word of God because, first, it was given by God through that special work of the Spirit called *theopneustia* (inspiration); second, its message, which emerges through the light that one passage throws on another, is God's word to the world; third, God speaks in and through this message to men's hearts. The Holy Spirit is the Bible's inspirer (by moving its authors to write what God wanted written to convey his truth), its identifier (by enabling the church to recognise which books were given to be canonical), and its interpreter (by showing Christians how the various elements of divine-human testimony in Scripture bear on their lives). The thinking of the biblical writers about God is taken as both source and control for ours; Scripture is enthroned as Christ's royal proclamation whereby he declares himself and directs us; and reformation – that is, correction and renewal – by the Word of God is seen as the only principle of spiritual life for either churches or individuals.

The majesty of Jesus Christ

Evangelicals embrace the high Christology of the New Testament, which displays Jesus Christ as God incarnate and the second representative head of the race – God for man and man for God, as Barth put it. Evangelicals follow the New Testament in seeing Jesus' death as a sacrifice which covers sin, averts God's judicial anger, reconciles us to him and so redeems us from spiritual bondage and jeopardy. Evangelicals stress the Father's love in giving his Son to die and his power in raising Christ from the dead as proof that his sacrifice was accepted and his atoning work done, and they highlight justification – that is, God's once-for-all remission of our sins and acceptance of our persons as righteous for Christ's sake – as the basic blessing of the gospel, a blessing which becomes a personal reality through faith which closes with God's promise by coming to the risen Christ as Saviour and Master. Evangelicals see the directing of worship, trust, obedience and love towards the incarnate Son as a natural and necessary element in Christian piety, and they labour to exalt the Mediator and hallow his name in every way they can.

The lordship of the Holy Spirit

With the New Testament, evangelicals stress the sovereignty of the Spirit in giving understanding, evoking faith and assurance, inducing new birth, prompting prayer, creating fellowship, sustaining self-denial, changing Christians into Christ's moral image, empowering them for service, and quickening the church. The often-heard dictum that pneumatology (the doctrine of the Holy Spirit) is the Cinderella among doctrines may in the past have been true of other traditions, but it has never been true of evangelicalism, which has characteristically viewed the Christian life as life in the Spirit and the Christian church as the fellowship of the Spirit.

The necessity of conversion

Contrary to what is sometimes thought, evangelicals as a body have never demanded that every Christian should have undergone a standard conversion experience; they have known the truth of Richard Baxter's dictum that 'God breaketh not all men's hearts alike'. But they have insisted that every Christian will show the marks of convertedness – active trust in God and an awareness of having met God and been changed by him, so that now one lives a 'turned' life – and where these marks are absent, even in orthodox, respectable, baptised churchgoers, evangelicals do not hesitate to conclude that conversion is still needed: that is, a turning to God in which Christ the Saviour comes and takes possession of one's life. Max Warren called this concept of indispensable conversion 'the citadel of Evangelical doctrine', and wrote of it thus:

> Begin by considering what the Evangelical means by conversion and before you know where you are you are face to face with the majesty and holiness of God, the sinfulness of man, the divine compassion and the divine Redeemer, the new birth, the new life...
>
> When the Evangelical speaks of conversion, and works and prays for conversion, he is concerned to promote a direct encounter between the Holy God and some man, some woman. That he should be in any way instrumental to this end is one of the most terrifying and sobering experiences that an Evangelical can know. And yet very simply he believes that God works like that...
>
> And what is this conversion? It is something that God does, not man. No one ever yet heard a man who had experienced an Evangelical conversion say "I have converted myself". The verb is always in the passive, "I have been converted". Something has been done to me by another and that Other, God.[1]

---

[1] Max Warren, *What is an Evangelical?*, London, Church Book Room Press, 1944, p. 23.

That is well said, and pinpoints what evangelical conversion is about. All that need be added is that in urging the necessity of conversion evangelicals stress most heavily the sinfulness, guilt, inability and lostness of fallen man. Wrote Bishop J. C. Ryle of Liverpool, an outstanding evangelical leader of a century ago: 'fruit-bearing Christianity' (he meant evangelicalism, as the context shows) 'has told men that they are born in sin, deserve God's wrath and condemnation, and are naturally inclined to do evil. It has never allowed that men and women are only weak and pitiable creatures, who can become good when they please, and make their own peace with God. On the contrary, it has steadily declared man's danger and vileness'.[2] From this characteristic emphasis flows both humility as regards oneself and compassion as regards others – which leads to our next point.

The priority of evangelism

What the joy of being found does for an evangelical is to drive him out to find others. His wish to share Christ seems to him natural and normal. He knows himself to be under orders to go as a witness for Christ and make disciples (cf. Matthew 28:18-20; Acts 1:8; etc.), and he finds himself wanting to do it. Witness to others is to him one aspect of that responsive offering of heart and life to God which is the essence of worship. Peter says that God's people are to 'declare the wonderful deeds of him who called you out of darkness into his marvellous light' (1 Peter 2:10). When asked if these words relate to worshipping God or witnessing to men, evangelicals want to say, both, and to identify the second as an aspect of the first. Warren wrote that 'this instinctive outward looking attitude' makes the evangelical 'alert to the Spirit of God calling out to fresh endeavours, revealing new areas of human life untouched by the Gospel,' and affirmed (he was addressing clergy): 'If you and I are being faithful in our ministry we too are seeing visions and dreaming dreams and reaching forth to those which

---

[2] J. C. Ryle, *Principles for Churchmen*, London, William Hunt, 1884, p. 452

are without'.[3] Quite so.

The importance of fellowship.

The give and take of those who are in Christ as fellow-believers is for evangelicals vital to spiritual health, and is moreover the essence of church life. Evangelicals are sometimes thought to have a weak view of the church, but this is a misunderstanding. What is true is that they see the church as first and foremost a community and an organism, in which matters of organisation, hierarchy, ritual nicety and canonical correctness are secondary, and fellowship – realising togetherness, and ministering to others' needs – is primary. Evangelicals have a high view of the ordained ministry as a personal pastorate, but a higher view of the church as a corporate priesthood in which all have equal access to God and are equally called to serve.

Such is evangelical Christianity, both within Anglicanism and outside it.

4. Where we are today

We have said that the Anglican evangelical identity problem has to do with adapting to change. As we labour to adjust to rapid cultural and social shifts around us, it becomes possible to wonder, with some non-Anglican evangelical observers, whether our convictions and purposes have not so altered that, however much we go on calling ourselves evangelicals, the reality of our evangelical identity is now lost. It becomes possible too for the sense of novelty so to swamp our minds that we lose touch with our own first principles and cry, with the domestic newspaper at the 1977 National Evangelical Anglican Congress at Nottingham, 'How can we know where we are going if we do not know who we are? What is an evangelical? Tell us, somebody, please.' The last chapter outlined the unchanging distinctives of evangelical - that is, as I for one believe, biblical, mainstream, normal and normative - Christianity,

---

[3] pp. 20f.

and the short answer to the question: who are we? is that we are the folk who try to live and act for God as these distinctives dictate. But to see what that involves we must come closer to contemporary facts, and take note of what has happened to Anglican evangelicalism in this century, particularly in recent years.

From 1900 to 1930 it can fairly be said that, by and large, Anglican evangelicalism was sinking. Not that it always looked that way, in the early days especially. On December 15, 1909, the editorial in the *Guardian* (a dignified, non-party Church newspaper, now defunct) declared:

> A new Evangelical party is in process of evolution ... The new type of Evangelical is full of life and energy ... He is eager to take a full share in Church life, and to develop it, if he can, on his own lines. He studies, writes, publishes books, even popular booklets, of great ability and wide range ... He believes in Church order, in discipline; he is imbued with the conviction that he is a member of a real Divine Society. For a movement with such ideals there is a future.

At that time something like a quarter of Anglican parishes were professedly evangelical, and the Church Missionary Society was one of the wonders of the Christian world. But Liberal Catholic dominance, under a galaxy of brilliant leaders, especially after the first world war, plus many experiences of division and defection in the evangelical camp due to the inroads of liberal thought about the Bible and the Cross, turned the mood of hopeful enterprise into one of disillusioned pessimism. Evangelicals of the older type withdrew into adventist speculation, cultural isolation and theological stagnation, leaving it to the liberals, evangelical and catholic, to think out the Church's role in a changing world. Victory in the Prayer Book debates of 1927-28 was in a deeper sense defeat, for it established an image of evangelicals as blind enemies of all change and made their name mud in the Church for many years. 'When in 1918 ... that great missionary, Canon W. E. S. Holland, toured England,' wrote Bishop Christopher Chavasse in his Foreword to Max Warren's pamphlet cited above, 'he was told by bishop after bishop that the future of the Church lay with the Evangelical school of thought. Ten years later, he returned on furlough from India to this country to find Evangelicals weak and discredited. They had split over the Bible and the Prayer Book.'

The next thirty years saw Anglican evangelicalism, one might say, bumping along the bottom. In evangelistic and missionary zeal, in the hallowing of personal and home life, in devotion to the Articles and the 1662 Prayer Book, clergy and laity of the thirties and forties were exemplary, but too often their piety was individualistic, their political and social opinions paternalist and backward-looking, their churchmanship a sort of established Congregationalism, and their distrust of and disregard for biblical and theological scholarship almost pathological. The clergyman who stood up at an evangelical society meeting to say, 'Don't trust the bishops; they're wicked men,' and those who once tried to dissuade me from reading theology at the University lest I lose my faith, were not wholly untypical. But during the fifties pastoral and theological talent increased in both quantity and quality, largely through the work of the Inter-Varsity Fellowship among students; negative attitudes were revised, and a swing back from 'liberal' to 'definite' evangelicalism began. The Anglican Evangelical Group Movement and the Evangelical Fellowship for Theological Literature, the main 'liberal evangelical' organisations, languished while the Tyndale Fellowship for Biblical Research, an IVF satellite, flourished. 'Definite' theological literature began to flow. A controversy about 'our English fundamentalism' in the mid-fifties showed that Anglican evangelicals had recovered some vigour and clout in debate, and the fruitfulness of Billy Graham's 1953 Harringay crusade electrified many with its demonstration of the continuing power of a plain biblical gospel. Clearly, there was life in the 'old paths' yet.

In the later fifties many young people became evangelical Christians. But the Protestant element in evangelicalism, which had been potent for a century, causing Anglo-Catholicism to be seen as a Romanist wolf in sheep's clothing and the 1928 Communion office as a disguised Mass, did not grab them. What they valued in the evangelical heritage as they received it was its emphasis on the Bible, on simple gospel doctrines personally applied, on intimacy with Jesus Christ whose divine friendship and presence supernaturalises all life, and on close fellowship among his followers. But most of these younger evangelicals did not see the Prayer Book as sacrosanct, and themselves as the bastion of national Protestantism against Roman invasion, in the way that their predecessors had done. To them Roman Catholicism appeared simply barren, Anglo-Catholicism simply senile and Britain simply pagan, and evangelism was their passion. Their Anglican loyalty focussed less on the Church of England's official doctrines than on the plain fact that it was (as it still is) the best boat to fish from. The renewed interest during the fifties in Reformed theology and devotion touched only a few of them at anything more than surface level. Being activists rather than intellectuals (which is not to deny that many of them had good brains) they were more impressed by practical shrewdness than by theological strength, and they valued their own theologians more for the former quality than the latter. In this they contrasted strikingly with many of their non-Anglican evangelical contemporaries, for whom the Reformed revival came as both a summons and a source of strength to maintain traditional formulations of doctrine and church principles, and traditional polemical attitudes too, through thick and thin.

4.1.   *Resurgence*

The past twenty years has seen an unmistakable evangelical re-surgence in the Church of England, of which the Keele Congress of a thousand in 1967 and the Nottingham Congress of two thousand in 1977 were two of the more striking public indications. During the same period world-wide evangelicalism in all denominations drew together impressively, with men like Billy Graham, John Stott and Carl Henry spearheading the process, and Anglican evangelicals both gave help to the Lausanne Congress on world evangelisation in 1974 and gained help from it. The Keele and Nottingham statements and the Lausanne Covenant give a fair idea of what Anglican evangelicals today are after. In brief, it seems that what the *Guardian* said of evangelicals in 1909 has once again become true. The name of the game is evangelistic outreach for conversions, along with the 'evangelicalising' of the whole church at all levels for renewal, plus the quest for proper ways to express a quickened social conscience. The movement is predominantly youthful; it is flexible and innovative; it has behind it some scholars, some rejuvenated theological colleges and a commercially viable publishing trade in its own paperback and periodical literature, so there is a steady supply of up-to-date resources. 'Definite' evangelicalism in the Church of England has made a come-back, under God, and looks as if it is here to stay.

Some changes are observable: we should note three.

A shift in style

The first is a shift in *style*. As society has changed, becoming more casual and free-wheeling, more egalitarian and less hierarchical in outlook, so evangelicalism has changed with it. Evangelicals have largely forsaken the rather mannered and prim ways of their fathers for 'pop' styles in music, dress (including haircuts, or lack of them) and speech to men and God. Evangelicals prayed publicly in 'you-who' terms years before Series III services appeared, and it is they more than any who have claimed the guitar and the idioms of rock, folk and soul for the praises of Jesus Christ. Westward position, bright family worship and *ad hoc* liturgy of all sorts are now common, and the old passion for keeping as close as possible to forms and words from the Prayer Book is clearly spent. Older evangelicals find the changes grating for a variety of reasons, but the belief that they are necessary if worship is to attract and be real and significant today, at least to the younger folk, is clearly the dominant view.

A shift in spirituality

The second change is a shift in *spirituality*: that is, in the way that communion with God is viewed and practised. In Britain it is mostly evangelicals, and Anglican evangelicals in particular, who have been touched and invigorated by the charismatic stress on emotional freedom, spontaneity, ecstasy, glossolalic and prophetic utterance in the Spirit, miracles, spiritual gifts, dimensions and depths of healing, and varieties of God's communication to individuals as they open themselves to his love in the ministering body of Christ. To be sure, these emphases only reinforce elements that were there in the evangelical tradition before (though not always prominently or respectably, nor with the theological rationale that some charismatics give them). But by bringing them into the centre the charismatic reinforcement has effectively demoted and indeed elbowed away the zealous concern for 'sound doctrine', for continuity with the evangelical past, for personal and corporate purity of faith and life, and for a spirit of humble watchfulness against sin and self-deception, which formerly did so much to shape evangelical devotion; and by treating *as* normal rather than exceptional modes of God's dealing with us that are discontinuous with the natural and rational it has altered the temper of much evangelical piety, which formerly rested on the belief that we commune with God through the biting of our minds on his Word, that the non-rational in any form is suspect, and that it is near-fanatical to expect miracles with any frequency. Some urge that emotional charismatic corporateness, with its heightened expectations of divine intrusion, is justified by the New Testament and is a needed corrective of cerebral evangelical individualism; others reply that its own inner lopsidedness is in the long run hostile to virility and maturity in Christ. We need not here decide which view is truer, or whether (as I am inclined to think) there is truth in both; suffice it to note that the charismatic emphases have marked evangelical spirituality deeply.

A shift in ethics

The third change is a shift in *ethics*, from world-denial to world-acceptance (Charles Williams would have said, from the Way of negating to the Way of affirming images), and from social, political and cultural detachment to positive involvement in these areas for God's glory. A generation ago, 'separation from the world' and avoidance of 'worldliness' were (rightly) pressed as central to the Christian calling, and to explain what this meant a standard casuistry of recommended abstinences went the rounds, approximately as follows: Eschew theatre- and cinema-going, except to see Shakespeare and the classics; plays and films are trivial, and acting demoralises. Eschew ballroom dancing, for it is sexually inflaming (though folk and country dancing, which involves less physical contact, is all right). Avoid reading novels and general literature (except for history and biography) beyond what one's academic and professional tasks require, for it is a waste of time and can corrupt. Do not drink alcohol in public, for this stumbles weaker brethren, nor in private, for drunkenness is always a danger and Christians do not need alcohol to pep them up. Do not play cards or other games of chance, for Luck is an idol and gambling, however small the stakes, is a great vice. Females should cut out cosmetics, fancy hair-dos, bright clothes and depilatory treatment, for this shows sinful pride in outward appearance; one index of unearthly inner beauty is dowdy dress and a bun. With this, indeed as part of it, went a casuistry of the professions: be a minister, missionary, teacher or doctor if you can, but don't touch polities (a dirty game) nor the arts (a world of decadence). How seriously all this was taken by some of its professed advocates is doubtful, but there is no doubt that it was taught. Now, however, the pendulum has swung the other way. 'Worldliness' has come to be defined (more accurately?) in terms of godless motives rather than of doing this or that, and it is recognised that abuse of something does not take away its proper use, nor is the use of Christian liberty identical with lawlessness or licence. In place of 1 John 2:15 ('Do not love the world') and Romans 12:2 ('Do not be conformed to this world') the guiding maxims are Genesis 1:28 ('Subdue ... and have dominion', the so-called cultural mandate) and 1 Timothy 6:17 (God ... furnishes us with everything to enjoy'), and what appeared as barbarianism is giving place to something more like humanism as a view of life, with corresponding entry into fields of thought and action which were previously taboo. This change has touched English evangelicals as a body, but Anglicans most of all. Some regret it as decadent, lax and 'worldly' in the old sense, but most welcome it as true advance in the service of God.

4.2.   *Profile*

Significant bodies of opinion usually have a strong sense of corporate identity and strong inner links, and Anglican evangelicals
today are no exception. Their sense of togetherness and common
purpose is fed by local and national structures for meeting and
joint action (Diocesan Evangelical Fellowships, the Eclectic Society,
Church Society,   Church Pastoral Aid Society, the Church of
England Evangelical Council, local gatherings organised by Bible
Society and missionary society auxiliaries, recurring residential
conferences, etc.); also by literature which most of them read (the
weekly *Church of England Newspaper*, the monthly *Crusade*,
publications from Falcon Books, Grove Books,   Church Book
Room and Vine Books, Marcham Books, Hodder and Stoughton,
Inter-Varsity Press, etc.); also by their viewing certain folk as 'our
leadership', and saying of other folk who might have been thought
to come in that category, and maybe think they do, that they are
'not really with us'. Good or bad, these things make for cohesion.

Critics sometimes say that today's evangelical Anglicans are
utterly different from their fathers, but judging them by those
evangelical essentials which we spelt out in chapter 3, one is struck
most forcibly by the depth of continuity. That today's evangelicals
understand themselves and their faith in essentially the same
terms as did their fathers, and have essentially the same goals in
life and ministry, seems too plain to be denied.   But, just as a ship
can only stay on course as the steering is adjusted to meet wind,
tide, currents and other hazards, so Anglican evangelicals can only
stay on course - that is, steadily pursue the defined goal of
spreading pure Christianity, by God's power and for God's praise -
by responding with appropriate adaptations to what goes on in the
Church and the community around. This is the truth embedded in
Newman's dictum (so objectionable, in the form in which he
developed it) that to remain the same a thing must change often.

These adaptive responses must themselves be authentically
evangelical - that is, they must consist of biblical principles applied
as a means to fulfilling biblical purposes, and not be expressions of
acquisitive or accommodating pragmatism which has lost sight of

the end in view. On this all evangelicals would agree. But each new situation has to be evaluated in terms of its present ingredients and possible outcomes, and just because all men see all situations selectively, with different factors impressing different minds, evangelicals, attempting to apply the same principles of judgment to the same situation, still end up again and again with policy differences, just as politicians of the same party do: the root of the difference being, not varying principles, but partial vision. All that can be done about such differences is to discuss them, and see if any one debater can persuade any other that his estimate of the situation overlooks something. It is, in any case, a stimulus to thought to have different opinions flying round our ears, and the Holy Spirit who teaches us to love God with our minds could be disastrously quenched by total uniformity of views.

The following characteristics of Anglican evangelicals today, as compared with Anglican evangelicals fifty years ago, are however distinctive features of their profile.

Discriminating involvement in the Church's life.

This is something so natural, and so much to be expected, that it would not call for mention were it not that for half a century before Keele many evangelical clergy and congregations lived in a spirit of defensive isolation from the rest of the Church, and many non-Anglican evangelicals, knowing this, are sure that all Anglican evangelicals have a bad conscience about being part of the Church of England, and would like to leave it. But this is the opposite of what is true today. Evangelicals have a positive commitment to the Church of England, based on its formularies, its history (or at least, the history of the gospel within it), its ethos of tolerance and trust, its openness to the Bible, and its possibilities tomorrow. When asked, as they sometimes are, under what circumstances they would leave the Church, they find the question so remote from reality, and therefore hard to answer, as a husband working hard and fruitfully at his marriage would find it were he asked under what circumstances he would divorce his wife. Also, they see that for the past thirty years God has been increasing their stake in the

Church of England quite dramatically: perhaps a fifth of the clergy and parishes now have an evangelical commitment, as do a quarter of each year's ordinands, and perhaps half the Church's missionary work is in evangelical hands. Plainly, this is a time for renewed effort, not for contracting out. Since Keele, as during the decade before Keele in some cases, evangelicals have sought to share fully in the Church's inner life and debates, though not by any means as 'yes-men' to officialdom - as witness evangelical challenges in recent years to prayers for the departed in alternative services, to the proposed Anglican-Methodist Service of Reconciliation, to radical theology (so-called) in its various forms, and to naive euphoria about relations with the Roman Catholic Church. Latimer House itself is a resource-point for the formulation of constructive responses to official Anglican proposals, as well as for midwifing creative scholarship directed to present needs and perplexities on a broader front. That the Church of England leaves much to be desired, and needs to be reformed and renewed by God at many points is something on which Anglican evangelicals are unanimous. That they would rather preach, teach, live, work and pray for revival within the Anglican family than move elsewhere is something on which as a body they are agreed too.

Diversified vision and priorities.

Evangelicals, by reason of their stress on (not just the right, but) the duty of private judgment, have always been individualists to a degree; differences of temperament always produce different preferences and policies in all communities; and the fact of having reestablished themselves in the Church as a force to be reckoned with has bred among evangelicals a sense of success - a mood which is regularly the mother of fragmentation, wherever it is found. It is no wonder, therefore, that evangelicals appear a good deal less cohesive a constituency than they did a decade back, and speak of themselves increasingly as a coalition rather than a party. The sense of common purpose in the Keele statement far exceeds that of the Nottingham statement, in whose seventy-odd pages the Articles are not mentioned once and, as is well known, cracks at the most unexpected points had to be papered over by verbiage.

(Whether it was wise to issue a statement from Nottingham at all, and indeed to hold such a Congress at all, are proper questions, though not for treatment here.) Nor is it any wonder that in particular debates, such as those concerning Prayer Book revision and alternative services, or Christian communication to outsiders, there should appear something of a polarization between 'conservationists' and 'innovationists', advocates of the dignity and depth which Anglican worship has achieved hitherto, and which demands language that is 'different', and protagonists of thorough-going identification with the thought and speech of the man in the street, even if that means settling for shallowness and loss of power. (No wonder either that exponents of both viewpoints should find the Series III compromises on this issue manageable without being in the least exciting - average liturgy, largely inoffensive but gawky and flat as a pancake.)

Nor is it surprising that, whereas progress so far makes some evangelicals increasingly anxious to press on and 'evangelicalise' the Church of England further, it has led others to settle contentedly for what they have got, so that now they 'make their contribution' to the Church without concerning themselves as to whether further and deeper changes in its ways are not now called for. Thus, while the total number of evangelicals in the Church increases, the number of campaigning evangelicals seems to decline. Whether this calm mood shows strength and statesmanship or sluggishness and myopia will be disputed. Linked with the calm mood, perhaps, is the fact that though there is much faithful pastoral care and outreach and great zeal to serve God (no doubt about that), today's Anglican evangelicals seem to have little prophetic vision about anything. Their effervescence often strikes the observer as bland and boyish, and complacent and naive to a degree - with exceptions, to be sure; but the exceptions are precisely not the norm. There was more vision and passion for the renewing of the Church to be seen in the sixties than can be detected now. Are the still waters running deep, or are they simply stagnant? Time will tell. But meantime, we note that here is another way in which evangelicals have diversified among themselves.

Dialogue with other positions.

A generation back, evangelical Anglicans by and large were in dialogue - that is, conversation taking both the topic and the other man seriously - only with each other and with fellow-evangelicals. When they listened to other professed Christians, it was not so much to learn from them as to controvert them and put them straight. The shadow of an unlovely intellectual perfectionism and self-sufficiency lay across this habit of mind; one can only be thankful that nowadays increasingly evangelicals listen to others in hope of benefiting by the exchange, as well as of sharing what they know with the other party. Their conviction (echoed, of course, by Roman Catholics and others, explain it how you will!) that God has given them a deposit of truth to guard, and their resolve not to let it slip away or be relativized or distorted, surely merits praise, but the assumption (hidden, yet potent) that evangelicals really have all the truth, and that God would never show Catholics or non-conservative Protestants anything that he had not first shown to evangelicals, making it needless for evangelicals ever to learn from those quarters, was really absurd, and it is a mercy that it is now so largely a thing of the past.

Some are puzzled that Anglican evangelicals should ever be found in dialogue with such as Roman Catholics, for officially Rome is committed to a long series of anti-evangelical positions (justification by baptism, transubstantiation and the mass-sacrifice, papal primacy and infallibility, the infallibility of the church and its identity with the papal communion, the immaculate conception and assumption of Mary, etc.), and since infallibility entails irreformability there is no apparent hope of change. But when individuals recognise a duty to explain and justify church doctrine from the Bible, as most Roman Catholic theologians nowadays profess to do, and the Orthodox and Anglican catholics always did, there is a basis for much fruitful conversation by qualified persons, and who knows what will come out of it? The recent Open Letter on Anglican relations with the Roman Catholic Church and other non-reformed Churches, which Latimer House sponsored, and the paperback *Across the Divide* (by R. T. Beckwith, G. E. Duffield and

J. I. Packer: Lyttelton Press, 1978) may be referred to here, as giving evidence of both the warrant for and the worthwhileness of exchanges of this kind.

5. Living with the Problem

Anglican evangelicals have an identity-problem today because the whole Church of England has one. It is important to see this. At bottom the problem concerns doctrine. One would naturally hope and expect that in any Christian body having the size, status and resources of the Church of England doctrinal understanding would deepen over four centuries, and it would be ridiculous, indeed a denial of the promised ministry of the Holy Spirit as teacher, to expect doctrinal understanding anywhere simply to stand still for so long a period. But the way in which doctrinal discussion has developed in the Church of England, particularly in this century, has brought deep perplexities. A glance at the history will explain this.

The Church's sixteenth-century Articles and Prayer Book (for the 1662 book is just a light revision of Cranmer's 1552 book, as reinstated with three small changes in 1559) exhibit a reformed Augustinianism, carefully guarded against Roman Catholic and Anabaptist deviations. The Articles first spell out the Trinitarian and Christological faith of the ecumenical creeds, which are themselves commended not as traditional but as scriptural (I-V, VIII). Then the Articles articulate and apply six main Reformation theses, as follows:

(1) Holy Scripture is sufficient for salvation and must be supreme in the church (VI-VIII, XX, XXI, XXXIV;   cf. XVII, XXII, XXIV).

(2) Fallen man's natural state is one of guilt, corruption and moral and spiritual inability (IX, X).

(3) Justification, which is by faith only through Christ only, belongs to that total salvation which flows to us through divine power from its source in God's gracious predestinating choice (XI-XVIII).

(4) Any company of believers among whom word and sacraments are duly ministered are God's church made visible (XIX).

(5) The sacraments of the gospel become means of the grace they exhibit by inducing faith in the Christ who instituted them, and to whom they point (XXV; cf. XXVI-XXIX).

(6) Since Christ's atoning sacrifice is a finished work, the eucharistic memorial of it is in no sense identical with it (XXXI).

Prayer Book devotion expresses these positions liturgically.

Prior to this century there was domestic debate, on and off, on four questions which arise when interpreting the Articles. The first was the extent to which tradition (however conceived and delimited) can be trusted as a guide to what Scripture means. The second was the nature of justifying faith, which some Anglicans have defined as in effect a meritorious work of commitment, guying evangelicals the while for teaching justification by feeling (i.e., by a feeling of being justified, which was how the critics mis-heard the evangelical doctrine of assured faith). The third was the effect of infant baptism, which some Anglicans saw as imparting a saving spark of divine life. The fourth was the sense in which in the eucharistic celebration Christ is present and the church offers sacrifice. But the outlines of Augustinian supernaturalism were not generally questioned in any radical way, though some 'Broad Church' descendants of the seventeenth-century Latitude-men had their doubts about original sin. No doubt Bishop J. C. Ryle, discussing the limits of comprehensiveness, was felt to be speaking from the middle of the Anglican road when he wrote in 1884;

> If ... a man calling himself a Churchman deliberately denied the doctrine of the Trinity, or the proper deity of Christ, or the personality and work of the Holy Ghost, or the atonement and mediation of Christ, or the inspiration and divine authority of Scripture, or the inseparable connection of saving faith and holiness, or the obligation of the two sacraments, I cannot understand what he is doing

in our ranks ... common-sense seems to me to point out that he cannot conscientiously use our Prayer-book, and that he has certainly no right to occupy our pulpits and reading desks.

(Principles for Churchmen, p. 37).

But since the twentieth century opened the Church of England has been having to ride out a whole series of storms raised by 'modernist' and 'radical' theologians, unruly children of English Broad Church and German liberal and existentialist Protestant parentage, who challenge the authority of the Trinitarian, Christological and soteriological thinking of the Bible at virtually every point. It is clear that the end is not yet, though it is also clear that since each such position is an unstable hybrid, the result of crossing current secular trends with current biblical hypotheses, none of them can last very long. Trends (fashions) and hypotheses (educated guesses) come and go, and whatever rested on them will go with them. (Who now recalls Rashdall, Major and Bishop Barnes? And does not Robinson's *Honest to God* already seem dated?) As Dean Inge saw and said, he who marries the spirit of the age will find himself a widower tomorrow. But what should be done about these heterodoxies during the short time of their blossoming? Anglicans, valuing scholarship, sure that truth is great and will prevail, remembering how Butler's *Analogy* put paid to the Deists of his day, and observing that Paul's initial reaction to error was to labour to correct it by argument, incline to hold that expert polemics, beating out the truth and exposing error for what it is, are the first thing to be desired, and hesitate to call for more action till the discipline of debate has had time to do its aperient work. It is evident that bishops in particular, despite their sometimes grandiose claims to be guardians of doctrine, hesitate to do more than hold the ring for debate, and when one thinks of possible consequences of a bishop withdrawing a clergyman's licence because he thinks the man is spreading mortal heresy one sees why. But the awkward fact remains that while the Church through its leaders merely holds the ring, what the outsider and indeed the ordinary worshipper sees is a licensed pluralism of belief about basics (which some present-day sophisticates would defend not as a necessary evil but as a positive good, a sign not of incipient breakdown but of rude health). And to anyone whose Anglican allegiance depends at all on what the Church of England is constitutionally committed to stand for, this state of affairs brings chilling bewilderment and a painful sense that the Church's integrity and credibility are both in process of being lost.

This is the heart of the Church's identity-problem as evangelicals see it, and of their own as members of the Church. Is essential Anglicanism an English form of international evangelicalism, as the Articles in effect say, or (in Ryle's words) is 'the Church a kind of Noah's ark, within which every kind of opinion and creed shall dwell safe and undisturbed, and the only terms of communion shall be willingness to come inside and let your neighbour alone?' (*op. cit.*, p. xxiv). Is Anglican comprehensiveness a matter of not insisting on more than the gospel as a basis of fellowship, or of not insisting on the gospel at all? No outsider could be blamed for concluding that it is the second, for that is what you see when you look at the Church today.

Time was when Prayer Book uniformity could be invoked as a witness to the essential evangelicalism of the Church of England, for the Prayer Book, as was said, turns into praise and prayer the biblical fundamentals pinpointed at the Reformation and set forth in the Articles. (It should be remembered that Cranmer, architect of the 1552 Prayer Book, was also responsible for the first draft of the Articles that same year.) Now, however, this move is no longer possible. There is less uniformity in Anglican worship today than at any time since the Reformation, for the Pandora's box of experimental worship is open, and no likelihood appears at present of its ever being closed. The official alternative services differ from those of the Prayer Book in at least one basic way: Augustinianism being out of fashion, they 'go light' on the sinfulness, moral impotence, helplessness and lostness of man without God in Christ. They are brisk, bright services, touching on sin only perfunctorily. They are evidently not written for folk who want to tell God that the burden of their sins is intolerable - not, that is, for folk who have entered deeply and existentially (as surely Scripture leads us to do) into the spirit and self-awareness of Articles IX and X. But what one believes about grace, deep down, reflects what one believes about sin, deep down; so that Anglican worship has now become problematical to a degree, just as Anglican doctrine has, and one can no longer appeal to the Church's corporate worship as evidence that its corporate faith is that of the Articles. The Church's current worship leaves open the question, what Anglicanism is today, for the alternative services can mean more or less, according to what is brought to them.

The sense that the communion to which we belong might be called 'Anglican Amorphous', on the model of Alcoholics Anonymous, is increased when one notes how in the ecumenical field Church of England representatives talk unity in all directions with an evident passion for pragmatic adjustments – and say different things to different churches! I was once entangled in diplomacy (call it that) with a man who regularly said different things to different people, as means of manipulating them. When the people started comparing notes, it became traumatic for both them and him. It pains evangelicals to see the Church of England inclined to behave that way – but of course nothing else is possible when basic Anglicanism has become fluid, and one man's idea of it is as good as another's.

Has the present pluralistic phase of Anglicanism come to stay, or is it a bad patch that the Church may in God's goodness come out of? Time alone will tell, but meantime the anxiety of thoughtful evangelicals, for whom the former alternative would be anathema, is and cannot but be acute. What are they to think of the empirical Anglicanism with which, according to Keele and Nottingham, they have so largely identified? The organisational pot –parish churches, bishops, the ordained ministry as a profession, diocesan quotas, etc. – remains without much change; but what strange brew is boiling up inside it? If the Christianity of the Church of England is in process of becoming something different from the dogmatic evangelical faith of the Articles, is not deep involvement in the set-up a bit perverse? And are not evangelicals themselves being changed in their sense of direction and their power to stand for the old paths? It is said that frogs in water that is being slowly heated show no awareness that their environment is changing, and no apparent discomfort, till suddenly movement stops and they are dead; may Anglican evangelicals be in a similar fatal process even now? This fear, as was hinted earlier, is widely felt, and some non-Anglican evangelicals of undoubted good faith play on it, thinking to awaken their Anglican brethren to their real peril before it is too late. Our remarks so far have been aimed at throwing light into the dark corners where this fear lurks. It is time now to draw the threads together in some closing points about how we should live with our situation as described.

5.1.   *Understand the psychology*

First, we Anglican evangelicals must *understand the psychology of our felt identity problem.* Bewilderment and a sense of disorientation regularly results from being caught in situations where various things are changing together, so that the mind must handle several variables at once. For me at least, the physical counterpart is the spinning head I get from the conjunction of simultaneously changing sequences of coloured lights in amusement arcades. As in my schooldays, as a brightish boy regularly defeated by maths, I would feel desperate and long to run away when my algebraic equations seemed to contain more undefined quantities than one could possibly determine (probably they did not, in fact, but that is how they seemed), so now in the Church of England, where a lot is changing at once, many feel panic and an impulse to run, for the situation seems out of control. The acuteness of our panic will vary, depending on how strongly our minds and hearts have taken up with the mental image of a constitutionally established Church of England which by rights should be as unchanging as God ('as it was in 1662, is now and ever shall be ...'): Anglicans who were less idolatrous at this point can cope with change better. But this is my point: the easiest thing in the world is to interiorize this panicky feeling, and say that we feel swamped in the Church of England, and at sea, and like fish out of water, and honestly to think we have lost our grip on our evangelical identity ('What is an evangelical? Tell us, somebody, please'), when our only real problem is that we find it hard to apply our familiar and firmly-held principles to what is going on around us. It may be, of course, that in the euphoric years since Keele some of us attended more to secondary things and theological hobbies and less to evangelical basics than was good for us; maybe our failure to reaffirm those basics at Nottingham testifies to this. Yet it seems clear that any sense of having lost touch with our evangelical identity is the emotional equivalent of an optical illusion. What is true is that we face a massive task of responding to changed and changing situations, which we must now get on with, as Nottingham rightly saw. Which leads to our next point.

5.2. *Positive evaluative biblical thinking*

Second, we Anglican evangelicals must *affirm our identity by positive evaluative biblical thinking about our Church situation.* Mental passivity in face of change ('I give up'), and jumping on band wagons because they are fashionable, are alike bad evangelicalism - bad stewardship, that is, of the truth entrusted to us to live by. For evangelicals live under a principle of authority - the rule of God in Christ through his Word interpreted by his Spirit - which requires them to 'test everything' (1 Thessalonians 5:21) by allowing the God-given Scriptures to teach, reprove, correct and instruct in righteousness in relation to it (2 Timothy 3:16 f.). Evangelicals' first loyalty is not to the Church of England as a going concern, to its 'mind' or any item in its tradition, but to the Word of the Lord and the Lord of the Word. As men under this authority they are Anglicans partly, at least, because they see the Church of England bound by its foundation documents to live under the same authority, understood in the same terms, and as capable still, despite its constant and chronic derailments, of being brought to obey that authority more perfectly. At least, the Church places no restraints on those who seek to persuade it to go that way, and, as we have seen, evangelical strength in the Church of England has grown considerably in recent years. But now it is for evangelicals, with their Bibles in their hands, to use their liberty responsibly by positive critical evaluation of the Church's present state and positive corrective proposals for the future.

This will involve grasping nettles - that of doctrinal discipline, for instance. Assuming what was said earlier about the need for scholarly debate against false views, what is the next step if the erring party proves incorrigible? If debate has sufficiently discredited his ideas in the Church's eyes, no more may be needed; but if not, and he is a clergyman and declines to resign, then some application of the 'non-reception' principle of 2 John 9-11 would seem to be called for. A. P. Baker quotes some words of John Stott:

> What should we do with heretics? ... I do not myself think a heresy trial is the right way. Heretics are slippery creatures. It is not easy to hook them. But is it too much to hope and pray that some bishop sometimes will have the courage to withdraw his licence from a presbyter who denies the Incarnation?

'No', comments Baker, 'it is not too much to hope and pray (and not only the denial of the Incarnation; what about the denial of the physical resurrection of Christ?). How can the Church of England remain in the least credible if there is no discipline for even the most major heresies, and how can Evangelicals remain credible within it if they do not press for such discipline?'

(Reformed Anglican Bulletin. October 1977, p. 14).

Now the Church of England Evangelical Council has produced a pamphlet entitled *Truth Error and Discipline in the Church* (London, Vine Books, 1978) which contains this sentence:

> In the last resort (i) if a central Christian doctrine is at stake, (ii) if the clergyman concerned is not just questioning but denying it, (iii) if he is not just passing through a temporary period of uncertainty but has reached a settled conviction, and (iv) if he refuses to resign, then we believe the bishop ... should seriously consider withdrawing his licence or permission to teach in the church.

Here is one example of consistent biblical thinking in relation to one of the Church's present problems. More such thinking is called for.

5.3. *Seeking spiritual revival*

Third, we Anglican evangelicals must *affirm our identity by seeking spiritual revival in our Church.* A. P. Baker notes that the 'in'-word today is renewal, 'meaning a kind of general revamping of local church worship, fellowship and structures to meet the needs of the present day. This is fair enough' (he continues) '... but it is dangerous if it becomes a substitute for Revival - that intensification by the Spirit of every part of His work in the life of the church, known above all by the presence of God Himself, and leading first to repentance among his people' (*op. cit.,* p. 16). Surely Baker is right. Only the notion of revival, thus conceived, is wide enough to express what biblical Christians should be seeking in the Church of England today.

With our one-track minds, we tend always to isolate this or that for exclusive consideration, and to talk as if the doing or stopping of some one thing was a complete prescription for the restoring of full spiritual health. But this is like prescribing for an invalid a diet consisting wholly of butter or syrup of figs. Butter is a rich and nourishing foodstuff, and syrup of figs has its use, but you cannot live on either. Similarly, you would be wrong if you urged that more (or less) worship revision, pastoral reorganisation, charismatic experience, ecumenism, social action, evangelical bishops, or whatever, was a panacea for the Church's present malaise: not because no single one of these things is part of the story - some of them are - but because you would be treating whichever you selected as the be-all and end-all of spiritual recovery, which it is not.

As an evangelical trying to interpret what I see by Scripture, I am forced to believe that the Church of England is under judgment in these days for multiple unfaithfulness to the gospel, and that our overmastering need is for God to revive his work, and in wrath remember mercy (Habbakuk 3:2; Psalm 85:4-7); and that we should be seeking his face constantly for just this (cf. Psalm 44; Isaiah 64). I doubt whether any but evangelicals will endorse this emphasis, and I urge that maintaining it is one vital way in which our distinctive evangelical identity should find expression at the present time.

6. For Further Reading

REPORTS

Christian Believing: Doctrine Commission of the Church of England (London: SPCK, 1976).

Keele '67: the National Evangelical Anglican Congress Statement (London: Falcon, 1967).

The Nottingham Statement: official statement of the second National Evangelical Anglican Congress (London: Falcon, 1977).

Truth Error and Discipline in the Church: Church of England Evangelical Council (London: Vine Books, 1978).

BOOKS AND PAMPHLETS

Balleine, G. R., *A History of the Evangelical Party in the Church of England*, new ed. with supplement by G. W. Bromiley (London: Church Book Room Press, 1951).

Beckwith, R. T., Duffield, G. E., Packer, J. I., *Across the Divide* (Basingstoke: Lyttelton Press, 1978).

Buchanan, C. O., Mascall, E. L., Packer, J. I., Willesden, Bishop of, *Growing into Union* (London: SPCK, 1970).

ed. King, John C., *Evangelicals today* (Guildford: Lutterworth, 1973).

ed. Packer, J. I., *Guidelines:* essays in preparation for Keele (London: Falcon, 1967).

Ryle, J. C., *Principles for Churchmen* (London: William Hunt. 1884).

ed. Stott, J. R. W., *Obeying Christ in a Changing World:* essays in preparation for Nottingham (London: Collins, 1977, 3 volumes).

Stott, J. R. W, *What Is an Evangelical?* (London: Falcon, 1977).

Warren, Max, *What is an Evangelical? An Enquiry* (London: Church Book Room Press, 1944).

ARTICLES

Baker, A. P., 'After the Ball was Over ...', *Reformed Anglican Bulletin*, October 1977, pp. 10-18.

Marchant, G.C.J., 'The Unshakable Things will be Left', *Churchman*, April 1977, pp. 114-23

The Evangelical Anglican Identity: The Connection Between Bible, Gospel & Church

by N. T. Wright

first published 1980

Latimer Study 8: Contents

Introduction

'WHAT is an Evangelical? Tell us, somebody, please!' With these plaintive words, written during the 1977 Congress of Evangelical Anglicans at Nottingham, John C. King (a former editor of the Church of England Newspaper) gave new impetus to the continuing search for Evangelical Anglican Identity. In the months that followed, this search was referred to by some as a 'crisis', by others as a 'problem', and by others again as a figment of introspective imagination. As the months have tuned into years, the latter judgment has been weakened as the debate has continued in the church press, at the Islington conference, and in various pamphlets and articles, notably the first in the present series of studies (J.I. Packer, *The Evangelical Anglican Identity Problem: an Analysis,* Latimer Studies no. 1, Oxford, 1978). Though there may be some whose personalities and parishes are so well-adjusted that they see no problem, *prima facie* there appears to be one.

What sort of a 'problem' is it? I do not believe the debates have been primarily about *aims:* we all agree (as do all Christians, surely, whatever 'label' they may adhere to) that our objective is the glory of God, the furtherance of the gospel of Jesus Christ, and the consequent need for personal and corporate holiness. No, the debated area concerns instead our *presuppositions* and our *methods* in achieving those aims. And this inevitably causes a certain amount of suspicion, so to speak, within the family. A is suspicious of B because he seems to have a different view of the Bible: B returns the compliment because A cheerfully wears a stole to administer Communion (and perhaps, to make matters worse, calls it 'presiding at the Eucharist'). C is suspicious of D because he is so involved in the wider Church of England, teaming up with non-evangelicals, and D of course fears that C, with all his work in interdenominational societies, hardly believes in the church at all. E and F are still having their cold war over liturgical revision; G and H are still debating the relative importance of truth and experience (or, if you like, the dangers of 'dry doctrine' and 'mindless enthusiasm'). And, to crown it all, when Dr. P stood up and said

75

that this constituted an Identity Problem, X, Y and Z accused him of unnecessary trouble-making. The frustration is actually increased by the fact that these alphabetical debaters are usually on excellent terms with each other: suspicion has not broken deep bonds of fellowship and love, and it is emphatically from this position that the present essay is written. We may have a Problem, but it is hardly a Crisis. Nevertheless, it would be a splendid thing if this log-jam could be shifted.

But log-jams, once formed, are not usually shifted by pulling and pushing at individual logs. What is needed may be a small explosion somewhere in the middle, to break up the jam and get things moving again. Such an operation may be a bit risky, both for the logs and for the person who lights the blue touch-paper, but it may be necessary: and this study is an attempt to have a go. What I intend to do is, first, to analyse where the blockage lies, with the help of a recently conducted Questionnaire (sections 1 and 2): then, having isolated some at least of the problems, to put underneath them a charge in the form of a restatement of the Biblical gospel to which evangelicals are committed (section 3): and then, lighting the fuse, to stand back and see what happens (sections 4-6). In the nature of the case, this sort of job needs to be done by individuals, and that creates a certain danger: though the truths to be restated are old and well-rounded, the very act of restatement must be provisional and not claim a definitive status. It is simply intended as an unblocking exercise.

Part of the difficulty is that the problems of which people are aware, at least at a popular level, are often not the real issues, but only symptoms of them. Thus (for instance) worries about the Bible go back to the old question of Authority: liturgy and clerical dress only worry people because they raise much deeper questions about the sacraments and ministry: the battle of 'unsound synods' versus 'interdenominational Evangelicalism' is really all about the nature of the church. John Stott's answer to the question with which we began was that Evangelicals are Bible People and Gospel People. But evangelical *Anglicans* have always felt that in some sense they are also *Church* people: and it is in the interaction between Bible, Gospel and Church that most of our current problems lie. If we can shift these central logs so that they stop getting in each other's way and float in their proper positions, the other logs wedged round the outside may start moving as well. (Perhaps I should add that when I worked on a lumber camp in British Columbia twelve years ago, the sort of operation I have described did *not* fall within my sphere of competence.)

1. A Tale of Two Circles

As soon as we try to line up Bible, Gospel and Church we realise that there are different models, often subconscious, of how being an Evangelical and being an Anglican are related. The question can be posed diagrammatically by drawing four different positions which are currently adopted: we will argue at the end of this essay that all are defective to some extent, and we will suggest a different one.

　　i. The first position is that of *Dogmatic Exclusivists*, and looks like this:

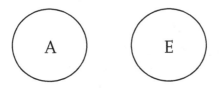

This is the classic free-church Evangelical position, represented by those, like Herbert Carson in his *Farewell to Anglicanism*, who have felt in all conscience that the two circles do not intersect, and that therefore if one belongs to the one one cannot ultimately belong to the other. This point of view underlies a good deal of the criticism of *Growing into Union* and of Evangelical theologians on the last Doctrine Commission (see Packer, *op. cit.*, pp. 29, 45 above). Comprehensiveness, according to this view, means compromise, and an evangelical can only be an Anglican if, by refusing co-operation with non-evangelical Anglicans, he implicitly denies that he really belongs in that church at all. (There have, of course, been many evangelical Anglicans who have done just this, just as some Anglo-Catholics have declared unofficial UDI from unsympathetic dioceses.) The really honest thing, it is said, is to 'come out and be separate'. One of the curious things about those who hold this position is that they insist on looking at the Church of England as it actually is, not as it professes to be in its formularies: whereas, facing Roman Catholicism, the same people insist that whatever Rome may look like today *her formularies have not changed*, and she is therefore not to be flirted with. Heads I win, tails you lose.

2. The second position is that of the *Establishment Inclusivists*, who regard Evangelicalism as one emphasis within Anglicanism, like this:

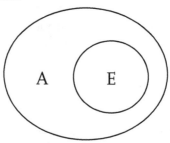

This view would not be held by many evangelicals, just as the first would not be held by many Anglicans: but it is important as one of the available options. Many Anglicans believe that, while there are few good reasons for remaining outside the Anglican fold, there are some good reasons for not being an Evangelical: and they therefore see Evangelicalism as one contributory factor within the wider church, merely one part of the 'Anglican Synthesis' (see the symposium under that title, edited by. W.R. F. Browning, Derby, Peter Smith, 1964). Though in many local instances this may have some plausibility, Evangelicals feel patronized by this attitude and often resent it, as though they were pet dogs kept in a kennel because they were good at barking when occasion demanded. On the contrary, they would reply, if we are right at all our emphases cannot be part of a different whole, but must be central.

3. The traditional Evangelical response would therefore be that of the *Idealistic Constitutionalists*, which looks like this:

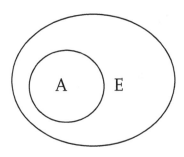

According to this view, the Anglican church *is* evangelical, as the Articles and the Prayer Book testify, though of course evangelicalism is present in other denominations as well. We are (so this view holds) not evangelical Anglicans (churchmen who happen to be gospel-men) but anglican Evangelicals: if the church changed her formularies to exclude the gospel we would go elsewhere. This is just as much a polemical position as the first, since its raison d'etre in the anglican communion appears to be that Anglicanism in reality is very different from what it at present seems to be: so that, while Evangelicalism has nothing new to learn from Anglicanism, the Anglican church should 'evangelicalize' itself if it is to be true to its basic nature (see Packer pp. 42, 44, particularly his phrase 'campaigning Evangelicals', p. 61 above). Needless to say, a good many Anglicans would oppose this vigorously, and many evangelicals find it difficult to hold such a view today because of the apparent gulf between the ideal Anglicanism envisaged (with all its members belonging also to international and interdenominational evangelical Christianity) and the actual present state of the church. Indeed, I suspect that part of our Identity Problem arises precisely because we have grown up with this model and have found it less and less satisfactory. We have climbed up a steep mountain path as 'campaigning Evangelicals', encouraging one another with the vision of the glorious summit that awaited us, only to find that we have arrived instead at a plateau with no summit anywhere in sight. We have attained numerical strength, synodical representation and respectability (not necessarily in a bad sense or for the wrong reasons) and the expected evangelicalization of the church has not taken place. Faced with this anti-climax, some of the mountaineers give themselves to finding a comfortable place to rest, glad that the climbing is over: others set about finding new tasks to occupy their energies, adapting their climbing skills to their new surroundings: while others feel decidedly uncomfortable, and organise Old Climbers Associations where the glorious conquests of former times are relived. This study intends to do none of these things, but to suggest that, at present hidden in the mist, there are new heights waiting to be scaled. For the moment, however, we must draw the fourth option taken by some today, corresponding to those climbers who look for a new role and new tasks.

4. Here the circles simply interlock, with anglican Evangelicalism (and vice versa) as the shaded area in the middle: its adherents are not so much campaigners, more *Contemporary Realists*.

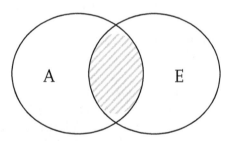

Those occupying this shaded position would assert that you don't have to be an Anglican, but it probably helps: this may be simply pragmatic (the 'best-boat-to-fish-from' argument, depending on the assumption that even if people don't go to church it's probably the C of E they don't go to) or more theological (we recognise that the New Testament has a high view of the church, and Anglicanism seems to be the best available way of combining this with a high view of the Gospel). Seen the other way round, this position implies that you don't have to be an evangelical to be an Anglican (the attempt to believe that the majority of Anglicans are in fact something different is too hard to sustain), but again it helps — presumably on the *historical* grounds that the Articles and Prayer Book point this way, and on the *theological* grounds that Evangelicalism is concerned with the central gospel truths of Christianity, which are not a mere party emphasis but essential to the very existence of any church. An occupier of this shaded area would not mind very much whether he was called an evangelical Anglican or an anglican Evangelical: both the nouns describe a larger entity to which allegiance is due, and both the adjectives delimit the nouns in the appropriate way (see Packer p. 45 above). Though such a person would not be so devoted a 'campaigning evangelical' as the occupier of position 3, he would still wish that more of his fellow Anglicans, and perhaps fellow Evangelicals, would come round to his point of view. It is, after all, part of believing something to be true and right that one wishes others to share that belief. The position is not comparable with that, say, of a goalkeeper in a football team, who knows that the success of the team depends on the other players being something else.

2. Questions and Answers

It was against this background that a Consultation of anglican Evangelicals (and/or vice versa) was held in St. Paul's, Robert Adam Street, London, in October 1979. Over a hundred people, clergy and laity, were present and discussed two papers and the matters arising from them. In the single day of discussion it was hardly possible to get beyond the symptoms of the problem to the root causes. It became apparent that the difficulties were not simply caused (as some had suggested) by an age gap between older conservatives and younger radicals: indeed, there were quite a few Old Turks and Young Fogies present. Nor was it merely a question of traditional ideas and modern rethinking (whatever the age of the people concerned). Certainly there was, and is, tension over such things as the new liturgy, but this itself is merely symptomatic of deeper needs and feelings and hopes and fears which have so far remained only vaguely expressed, if at all. I was left with the feeling that real communication and discussion between many of the parties involved had still not taken place.

At this point some will feel that the whole exercise, including this commentary on it, was clearly irrelevant and time-wasting. We are bound to quarrel, it will be said, if we sit around looking at one another instead of looking up to God and out to the world. But this misses the point. The members of the Consultation were busy people, whose lives consist in doing, or trying to do, those two things, but who were and are concerned to do them in the spirit of Philippians 2:2 ('be of the same mind, in the same love, in full accord and of one opinion'): unanimity between fellow-workers is not an optional extra, but something in itself to be prayed for and worked towards. It is precisely because our corporate looking to God and witness to the world suffers when we are at sixes and sevens amongst ourselves that occasional attempts to sort things out are necessary.

In order to try and get to the root of the problem, therefore, the Church of England Evangelical Council (which had set up the Consultation in the first place) subsequently asked me to conduct a survey to prepare the ground for a second Consultation to be held in January 1981. This survey took the form of a questionnaire, sent to about two hundred people all over England: and the present section of this study is as near as can be got (in the nature of the case) to being a formal report of the results.

The survey asked six questions. The first two attempted to extract *priorities*: (i) 'What do you see as the points most needing to be stressed by Anglican Evangelicals today?' and (ii) 'What do you see as the greatest danger(s) for Anglican Evangelicals today?' The next two attempted to establish *underlying presuppositions*: (iii) 'What, ultimately, are you wanting to safeguard by your answer(s) to qu. (i)?' and (iv) 'What, ultimately, are you seeking to avoid or prevent by your answer(s) to qu. (ii)?. The last two sought to isolate fears and anxieties: (v) 'Why do you think some people attack or at least fail to emphasize the points set out in your answer to qu. (i)?' and (vi) 'Why do you think some people defend or promote the points mentioned in your answer to qu. (ii)?'

Though the matter might have been handled better if an experienced sociologist had drawn up the questions (some people answered the first two in such a way as to make some of the others unanswerable), several things emerged clearly enough to point up certain issues which must be thrashed out if evangelicals are to enjoy sufficient mutual understanding to make shared policies and action a reality.

With such wide-ranging questions it is clearly impossible to tabulate answers in any comprehensive way, and in any case statistics would be irrelevant to a proper theological evaluation of the various attitudes and beliefs, reflecting only the somewhat haphazard selection of recipients for the questionnaire. What matters are the issues which people have on their hearts. The best way of reporting back on the questionnaire seems therefore to be the (admittedly subjective) one of outlining these issues and commenting on the way in which they were raised. There are five areas emphasized again and again in the replies to the six questions.

2.1. *Why be an Evangelical, anyway?*

Perhaps the most basic problem is: do we *need* to talk about 'evangelicalism', to line ourselves up as a party, at all? One of the replies came from a staff member of a theological college, who said that his students were for the most part bored with the 'identity problem', and just wanted to get out into the parishes and preach the gospel. Others report a widespread feeling that we do not need to think of ourselves as 'evangelicals' at all, that such party spirit is needlessly divisive, perpetuating old and now irrelevant battles, 'campaigning' when there is no battle, or at least not *that* battle, to fight. It may well be that those who did not reply to the questionnaire – nearly half of those circulated – may have felt it irrelevant for just these reasons. Other replies, aware of this view, took issue with it, stressing the need for corporate thinking and action, and insisting that distinctive evangelicals continue to have a job to do until such time as the whole Anglican communion is 'evangelicalised'. (In other words, the 'campaign' must go on.) One Diocesan Missioner wrote of the misunderstandings which many have of the meaning of 'evangelical', and regretted the isolation from evangelical fellowship and thinking which occurred when young ordinands shied away from the label. It seems that at this level there is both need and room for a growth in mutual understanding: to reject the label 'evangelical' because one's desire is to preach the gospel becomes ridiculous as soon as the real meaning of the word emerges. (We may comment that many of those at theological colleges will discover when they are ordained that the church outside the college is a much stranger place than they imagine, and they will soon be looking for one or two like-minded folk also preaching a recognisable New Testament message in their areas ... and then the reality of the Problem will become all too apparent.)

The trouble is that the word 'evangelical', like a chameleon, has taken on fresh colour from its surroundings. Many younger Christians who are, more or less, at one with traditional evangelical belief and practice, have indicated that they reject the label because of the connotations (backward-looking traditionalism, party spirit and Prayer Book fundamentalism) which it has come to have in some quarters. It is clear from the replies to the questionnaire that many evangelicals, familiar with the term in happier contexts, find this reaction incomprehensible, and think that it betokens instead a wish to sit loose to the Bible or the Gospel – as in some cases it may do, but in many it certainly does not. Here are all the makings of a first-class misunderstanding. I hope that further consultation, involving particularly theological college staffs and students, will go some way towards clearing it up.

2.2. *Basic Doctrine*

By far the majority of the replies emphasised the importance of basic doctrine. Several underlined one or other of the fundamental truths set out by Dr. Packer (pp. 47–2 above), often stressing the centrality of the Scriptures and the Cross. Here we reach, I believe, one of the basic causes of the current problem. Many replies came from people who have spent twenty years or more working and praying to bring the Bible and the Gospel back to the centre of anglican life and thought, and who now feel that, with the battle almost won, these things are being lost sight of by the very people who ought to be picking up the tools and finishing the job. This is clearly a multiple problem, and needs further analysis. Many of the responses indicated a fear that the evangelical movement is in danger of splitting up along the lines of 'liberal evangelical' versus 'conservative evangelical', with the crucial issues being the Bible and the Atonement. (Those with long memories, or who have read the period up, think back to the similar splits earlier this century between the IVF (now UCCF) and SCM, and between CMS and BCMS.) Precisely because of the numerical strength of evangelicalism (for instance in the student world, where the Christian Unions (affiliated to the UCCF) are usually far larger than any other student Christian organisation) it is easy for those without a clear doctrinal commitment to find a home within what is in theory an evangelical organisation, and even to reach a position of leadership and responsibility within it. Nor is this always a bad thing: many are being 'evangelicalised' quietly and effectively who two generations ago would have run a mile at the thought. But some doctrinally conscious evangelicals, observing this happening, indicated by their replies to the questionnaire that they see it as a step down the slippery slope to a loss of distinct witness, under pressure from the desire for popularity in the church and the world.

The questionnaire was by no means the first occasion on which this fear emerged. It was present at the 1977 Nottingham Congress – sometimes, I think, justified, and sometimes emphatically not. There were some there who, though still wanting to be regarded as Evangelicals (why else were they there?) had clearly ceased to believe in Biblical infallibility in any recognisable sense, or in substitutionary atonement, and who had embraced (for instance) universalism. But there were others, myself included, who were trying (as paper-writers had been firmly told to by the organisers) to re-express standard orthodox evangelical theology in fresh and creative ways, and who were hauled over the coals as though they belonged in the first group, simply because well-known 'shibboleths' were (quite deliberately) avoided. Looking back now, I do not regret the experience, but I fear that the structure of the Congress, particularly the attempt to produce an all-embracing 'statement' virtually overnight, gave many participants entirely the wrong impression of what is going on elsewhere in evangelicalism, and perhaps itself contributed to the Identity Problem with which we are now faced.

2.3. Battles over the Bible.

Nowhere was this more apparent than in attitudes to the Bible. Several of the replies to the questionnaire expressed anxiety about the apparent 'creeping liberalism' which is reducing confidence in the written Word of God, among evangelicals and elsewhere. Some insisted on terms like 'inerrancy' or 'infallibility' while others made the point that these terms, themselves actually non-Biblical, need a lot of unpacking before they can become even meaningful. In many cases the questions of biblical authority and interpretation were raised in connection with key areas of doctrinal or ethical debate: if we *really* made the Bible central (said some replies) there would be no question about (e.g.) homosexuality or women priests. But (replied others) it all depends how you interpret words written in and for one age and culture when ours is so different. From the replies to the survey it is clear – as it was often not clear at the Consultation in October 1979 – that those who say the latter are not (certainly not necessarily) giving up the centrality of Scripture or 'going soft' on 'infallibility'. Talking about 'hermeneutics' is not an automatic indication of incipient liberalism, even if it is true, as many assert, that Scripture is currently under attack from a new wave of what used to be called 'liberalism', and that evangelicals, including some within 'our' colleges, are not immune to this.

2.4. God-centred Christianity

The same is true, *mutatis mutandis*, of the other doctrinal points which were made in answer to the first two questions of the questionnaire. The sovereignty and supremacy of God, the divinity and saving death of Jesus Christ, justification by faith, the necessity for the work of the Holy Spirit, the new birth and holiness of life, were all emphasized again and again. The corresponding dangers are seen by many to be man-centred religion, doctrine and worship, entered into because it is more comfortable and less likely to alienate people in the wider church. There are many ramifications to this position but the focal point has often been questions related to the incarnation. Some replies indicated unease at current attempts to use the humanity of Jesus as a theological peg on which to hang a new version of an old 'social gospel'. Others felt, conversely, that 'Docetism' (the heresy which so stressed Jesus' divinity as to make his humanity a mere illusion or pretence) has always been an evangelical weakness, and needs to be combatted at every level.

We may comment at this point that the problems have come in areas common to all evangelicalism. The danger of infiltration of liberal ideas is always present, and must be strenuously guarded against if the gospel we preach is to remain the genuine article. But the possibility of real wolves is no excuse for crying 'wolf' every time someone says something in a new way. If it is right to have a defensive strategy as part of one's equipment, it is important to ensure that the computers which warn of danger are functioning correctly. But, once that is said, the old enemy of liberalism remains as potent and present as ever, as powerful as the Spirit of the Age from which it draws so much. It will not always attack in the same place, but the long-term target will be the same – the definite, clear and compelling proclamation of the gospel. It is the voice of authentic evangelicalism which insists, in a great many of the replies to the questionnaire, that evangelism remains a top priority, and that the gospel in its essence remains unchanged from one generation to another.

2.5. *Protestant principles*

If 'liberalism' is one great traditional enemy of evangelicalism, the other has been (broadly speaking) Catholicism. Here the Identity Problem is quite different, and more complex. It surfaces in the results of the questionnaire in two apparently conflicting ways. On the one hand, many who wrote back are evidently dissatisfied with what they see as excessive individualism in evangelical theology (manifesting itself in the influence of interdenominational para-church organisations, methods of youth evangelism, etc.) and are struggling towards what they hope is a more biblical view of the church. This goes hand in hand with a new awareness of the importance of the sacraments and the ordained ministry. On the other hand, many fear a re-awakening of sacramentalism', 'priestcraft' and all that goes with it. Several write of dioceses or deaneries where apparently old-fashioned Anglo-Catholicism reigns supreme, where people are taught that coming to church and attending communion is all that is necessary to salvation, where the Bible is not being heard as the living word of God because the church is stifling it. These fears are sometimes obliquely supported by the current desire for 'every-member ministry' as opposed to the 'one-man bands' which have characterized so many churches (not just anglican) for so long, and which indicate (some would say) a clericalism which obstructs and impedes the gospel. The two positions outlined here – the one wanting to re-emphasize the church and sacraments, the other wanting to de-emphasize them– were sometimes aligned, in the replies to the questionnaire, with the doctrines of Incarnation and Atonement respectively.

2.6.   *Result: a Composite Problem*

Here, then, is the log-jam. So many different logs, indeed, are piled up that it is easy to see why a single day's Consultation was not long enough to do more than register a whole list of loosely related worries. I am aware that I have not represented here *every* position taken up, or point made, in the replies to the questionnaire, but I think most who wrote will recognise their concerns somewhere in the five sections above. What follows now is an attempt to do what the Consultation, and many who wrote in, were anxious to see: to rethink ideas in order to provide some new ways forward. It is thus in direct response to Consultation and Survey alike that the remainder of this study is conceived, looking ahead to the next Consultation at the start of 1981: though the principles set out here, if valid, will of course have wider implications than just helping to set the agenda for a single meeting.

Before we begin this difficult task, perhaps some words are in order about the ground rules (so to speak) for this kind of debate. It is characteristic of Evangelicals that they have a proper sense of stewardship for the truths of the Bible and the Gospel, and a healthy awareness that these truths are often under attack. But this right and proper sense, and awareness (which would be traced back at least as far as Paul's warnings to the Ephesian Elders in Acts 20), sometimes produce the unfortunate result that, in debate, one is always ready to believe the worst, to draw the most damaging conclusions from something someone else is struggling to say. Worse, 'stewardship' can be the cloak for quite different interests, personal, factional or whatever. But the cause of Christ is not served by suspicious inference or accusatory innuendo. Careful and generous dialogue, always ready to give the other person the benefit of the doubt, must be the order of the day: constant effort is needed to *hear* what is actually being said even if the initial impression may be startling. In particular, we are often dealing with complementary truths which have at times been regarded as contradictory: e.g. to stress the humanity of Christ is *in no way* to undermine his divinity (this is of course controversial within the wider current debate, but should not be so among evangelicals). So, too, no-one ever says in one contribution, spoken or written, all that is in his mind on the subject, but only the point(s) he or she thinks most need stressing at the moment. Evangelicals, not least the present writer, need to learn how to *love* one another in the context of theological debate.

What follows then, is an attempt to set a new context for such discussion, not to provide instant recipes or absolute solutions. It is one man's perspective, not a new party line or a piece of factional propaganda. It tries to look afresh at the Biblical Gospel and its relevance for the problems under discussion, and it needs response, suggestions, and where necessary correction if it is to achieve its aim.

3. The Biblical Gospel

With a heading like that, disclaimers are called for. This section is merely a pencilled sketch for a fuller picture, but it is vital that we have at least such an outline in mind before we start to see what the picture implies. At the same time, it is one of the truths which evangelicals love to proclaim that the biblical gospel is basically simple. 'Christ died for our sins, and was raised from the dead.' What more needs saying? Nothing, in essence: but a great deal by way of setting the simple statement in its context and drawing out its implications. Already these tasks have been begun when Paul adds the words 'according to the Scriptures' (1 Corinthians 15.3.f.). The effect of this is to set the central saving truths – the cross and resurrection – within the context of God's revealed plan, his authoritative account of his own rescue operation for the world, and to say 'these are the events to which, in a whole variety of ways, the Old Testament was pointing'. We begin, then, with the context of the Gospel: God's saving purpose, as revealed in Scripture.

3.1.   God's Rescue Operation

The significance of Jesus' death and resurrection can only be grasped if we realise that Jesus was taking on himself God's purposes for Israel. In the context of the Old Testament, the call of Abraham is God's answer to the problem spelt out in Genesis 3-11. Sin has entered the world: man has rebelled against God, and the world is in consequence out of joint: man is alienated from God (Ch. 3) and from his neighbour (Genesis 4, 11), and is in consequence lost and under judgment. Within this context God calls Abraham to be the means through which he will bless the world which at present lies under the curse: Abraham is to be the founding father of the family of salvation. And this task is progressively clarified as we move on through the Old Testament: Israel is to be a nation of priests, a royal priesthood, a holy people, representing the world to God and God to the world, called to be the light of the nations. Her prophets are raised up by God to speak his word to his people (even if the people rejected his will when they were told it): her priests are not in their own right mediators between God and the people, but God's appointed means of enabling his people to know that their sins were forgiven not by their own actions – nor by those of the priest – but through

God's grace. In particular, the King is to be the representative of his people, the one in whom Israel is summed up. But all through the Old Testament these truths are set out as paradoxes. God's covenant with Abraham, and with Moses, has not resulted in the salvation of the world, but has instead shown up Israel's own sin and failure. The line of kings does not rule in splendour and righteousness over a worldwide empire of justice and peace. Israel is unable to take her place as the key figure in God's worldwide saving plan. And when the plan reaches a climax in Isaiah 40-55, which expounds that covenant faithfulness of God because of which he will save the world through the suffering of his righteous servant, it becomes apparent that though the servant in one sense 'is' Israel, the nation herself needs redeeming just as much as the peoples of the world around.

God's rescue operation thus devolves on to Israel's representative. 'In the fulness of time God sent forth his Son' (Israel had been called God's son), 'born of woman, born under the law' (i.e. a true child of Adam, and of Israel) 'to redeem those who were under the law'. Jesus is anointed with the Spirit to be Israel's rightful King, the one in whom Israel is summed up, the one who can take Israel's task on himself and do, for her and for the world, what she could not do. *Why* he is able to do this we will see presently: *that* he does it is the message of the whole New Testament. He suffers, dies, is buried and rises again as the one who, representing Israel, is fully fitted to stand in her place: and because Israel was God's means of saving the world, her anointed King dies and rises in the place of the world also. The New Testament writers assert that Israel's destiny of vicarious suffering (which is still deeply embedded in Jewish consciousness to the present day) has been taken by one man as the climax of God's rescue operation for the whole world. Just as Judah offered to bear the blame, and the consequences, of Benjamin's (imagined) sin (Genesis 45: 18-34), so the Lion of Judah has stood in the place of all his 'brethren' the world over, and has taken upon himself the guilt, and the consequences, of their actual sin. The cross and resurrection are not to be understood in isolation, but as the final and all-important act in the drama which began with the call of

Abraham.

3.2. God's New People

If God's purpose in calling Abraham was to reverse the sin of Adam, and if that purpose has been achieved in Jesus Christ; then in Jesus Christ God has not only rescued sinners, but is planning to turn them into his true humanity, humanity at last as it was meant to be. When Jesus rose on the third day he rose with a body which, having passed through death, was no more subject to it (Romans 6:9 f.). Jesus has reconstituted humanity in himself. Sinful humanity died on the cross (Romans 8:3): true humanity, continuous with that sinful humanity but now purged by Jesus' death, rose on Easter morning. All those who belong to Jesus the Messiah therefore belong not with the sinful humanity but with the true, even though the fact that sin and death still have to be faced and beaten make this a paradoxical state to be in, with the Christian life being a matter of becoming, by the power of the Spirit, what one already *is* 'in Christ' (i.e. belonging to the Messiah's people), and what one *will be* fully in the resurrection. This is the picture which underlies Romans 5-8, which follows from Romans 1-4 as the statement of how, because of the work of the Messiah, Adam's sin and its consequences are reversed in and for the true children of Abraham (see ch. 4). At the same time, Israel – as the people of God, but also the people in whom Adam's sin is seen to its full extent because of the law (Romans 5:20) – is reconstituted just as humanity has been. The church rises on Easter morning in place of the Israel that has died on the cross: and all who want to belong to the reconstituted people of God must be joined to the Messiah, by baptism and faith, in his death and resurrection. This is the theological position underlying the argument of Galatians 2:14 – 4:7, which would repay detailed study at this point.

One of the features of this passage which we must here underline is that the new people of God, the redefined Israel, are still *the historical people who look back to Abraham as their chronological starting point*, precisely because they look to Jesus as their theological *raison d'etre*. The 'new covenant' of Jeremiah 31 and Ezekiel 36 has been established: God has, in Christ, reconciled the world to himself, providing that forgiveness of sins for which the Old Testament longed, and to which the Levitical sacrifices pointed. But the process of renewal has not meant abandoning the idea of an historical people: Paul's whole argument in Galatians 3 and Romans 4, and the statements of Matthew 3, 9, 8, 11 etc., assume that to be saved one must belong to Abraham's family. Instead, the family which had been constituted so as to be formed by flesh-and-blood descent is reconstituted so as to be formed by the worldwide mission of the church – an equally historical and visible programme, fulfilling at last the vocation of Israel to be the light to lighten the Gentiles. Israel, the family of Abraham, is at last becoming a worldwide people, characterized by the historical and visible fact of baptism (notice how baptism comes in precisely in this context in Galatians 3:27 and Romans 6:3 f.) and of course faith – faith, the sign that God's Spirit has been at work and that the person concerned is indeed a member of the new covenant family. (This is where the whole doctrine of *justification* comes in: see my paper in *The Great Acquittal*, ed. Gavin Reid, Collins, 1980). The historical mission of the church, whose mandate is detailed in Matthew 28:16-20, Luke 24:44-9, John 20:19-23, Acts 1:6-8 (cf. too Acts 9:15, Romans 15:8-13), depends theologically on just this fact, that in the death and resurrection of Jesus Israel has been reconstituted, has in fact been turned inside out.

3.3. God's Kingdom

Man, and Israel, are thus condemned on the cross and reaffirmed in the resurrection. In this double verdict lies the paradox of grace – that grace 'perfects' nature without abolishing it, but that this perfection is only achieved through death and resurrection. This is of profound importance for our subsequent sections. Different traditions within the church have tended (in effect) to force apart the cross and the resurrection, in two ways.

The first way insists on the discontinuity of the cross, on God's judgment on sin, on the impossibility of salvation through man, Israel or history simply proceeding as they are; this view, always bordering on Manichaeism (see Packer, p. 41 f. above), is suspicious of talk about an historical church, the renewal of humanity, and even (in radical protestant circles) the incarnation and resurrection (disbelief in which is thus not merely applied rationalism, but the outworking of a particular – arguably unbiblical – view of grace).

The second way is so concerned to stress God's work in the world, in the church, in history and in humanity that it sometimes talks as if man simply needed 'ennobling' in order to be fitted for salvation, as if humanity and history could simply be underwritten by grace, could be affirmed as they stand.

Though most Christians, perhaps, are sufficiently aware of the fuller picture to want at least some sort of compromise between these two ways, the extremes appear at first sight more thoroughgoing and hence more attractive, so that theologians have sometimes constructed schemes in which one side of the truth becomes simply a function of the other. Thus Bultmann, for example, so emphasized the cross, God's judgment on man, Israel, history and the world, that he left no room for incarnation, resurrection or the historical church in his scheme: the first two became 'mythical' ways of talking about the cross and its effects, and the last is an 'early Catholic' degeneration, a lapse into unChristian or at best subChristian ideas. Possible examples of the opposite mistake would be a 'social gospel' which failed to take account of God's judgment on sin, or which failed to see that in taking humanity Jesus took it to the cross, and imagined that mere social improvement, without the necessity of judgment, would bring in the kingdom of God: or an idea of 'pipeline grace' in which historical succession would automatically guarantee saving grace: or a devotion to the incarnate and glorified Lord which saw the Passion merely as a splendid example of selfless suffering. We will return to some of these matters presently.

In fact, cross and resurrection together are essential for God's purposes of salvation. God did not send his Son to condemn the world and leave it at that; nor to tell the world that it was all right and just needed improvement at a few points. He sent him to *redeem* the world – to submit the world, in himself, to the process of death and resurrection by which the world – humanity, Israel, history, the world of nature – might be saved. God's rescue operation is designed to put the world back into the running order it should have had from the beginning, not to scrap it and start something totally new. And for this purpose the reconstitution of *man* is central and vital, because man was made to be God's vice-gerent over the world (Genesis 2), and the world (correspondingly) was made to be itself and serve God's purposes when being ruled over by obedient man. The fall of man meant that God's sovereign rule over the world was only exercised paradoxically, with thorns and thistles and floods bearing witness to the fact that human sin had put the world out of joint. But within God's plan of salvation man is called once more to obedience, and the world in consequence is to be redeemed: the waters part for the Israelites to go through, the land will flow with milk and honey. History becomes 'salvation history': a human family becomes the people of God. Though Israel's sin means that these blessings are partial and paradoxical, they are real signs of the full gift of grace that is to follow: when the obedient Man comes he proclaims the Sovereign Rule, i.e. the Kingdom, of God. The central point about the proclamation of Jesus is that God is at last ruling the world through obedient man, as he always intended. That is why storms are stilled, and loaves and fishes multiplied, at his word. That is why demons are rebuked, lepers cleansed, dead men raised. In Jesus' ministry we catch a glimpse, albeit short-lived and localized, not just of his divinity but of humanity and the world as they were meant to be, and of Israel and the world as they were meant to be. Jesus comes to judge *and* save the world. In his total mission the world humanity, the people of God, the course of history and the world of nature – are submitted to condemnation *and* reaffirmation. The Kingdom of God comes not to abolish all these, nor simply to underwrite them, but to redeem them.

The Kingdom is not now present in exactly the same way as it was in the ministry of Jesus. No longer is there a totally obedient man walking the earth, with creation consequently totally subject to him. Nevertheless, though his people, the church, are less than fully obedient, they are spread in all the world, and the Kingdom which awaits fulfilment at his return sheds its light before it as the world is brought into submission, however partial, to the sovereign rule of God exercised through (even partially) obedient humanity. This light shines in different ways at all levels. As the church obediently witnesses to her Lord, preaching the gospel and living by it, the world is judged and redeemed: here is the theological programme for total mission. As the church lives by the grace given in word and sacrament, she becomes in herself the historical people of God, *semper reformanda* and *semper catholica*. As God's people exercise actual historical obedience in holiness and in suffering, history and the world are redeemed (cf. Colossians 4:5). As the Christian obediently 'puts to death' the deeds of the body, presenting it as a 'living sacrifice' to God, that 'body' – i.e. that whole personality, including particularly its physical aspects – becomes truly human. The world, the church, history and the individual are thus brought into a continual process of death and life, of judgment and salvation, all stemming from the central events of Jesus' death and resurrection. In particular, God's gift of prayer is the sharply focussed point of the Kingdom: in the prayer which the Spirit gives, the 'people of God' take their place as obedient to God and sovereign over the world (cf. Romans 8:26 f.). God has willed to rule the world through obedient humanity: and prayer is the closest we ever come on earth to realizing that purpose, which will be fulfilled in the final resurrection. Prayer is, in fact, one more sign of inaugurated eschatology, of the beginning of the End in Jesus Christ and his people.

This whole range of thought, reflected all through the gospels and summed up in such passages as Romans 5:12-21 and 8:1-30, 1 Corinthians 8:5-6 and 15:20-28, Ephesians 1:3-23, Philippians 2:5-11 and 3:2-21, Colossians 1:9-23, allows us to return to our starting-point and reflect on the eternal saving purposes of God. Within the confession that Jesus, the Messiah, is Lord, the church acknowledges him as the true sovereign over the universe, who takes the place intended for man from the beginning and thus, since humanity was made for him in the first place, takes at last his own rightful place, enters into his true inheritance, becomes manifest as the Lord of the World, which he was from the beginning. Here is the centre of the Gospel. God made man to be Lord of the world so that his eternal Son, the Word through whom and for whom all things were made, should become manifest as Lord of the world by becoming true Man. God created Israel to be the means of saving the world, to be his true humanity, so that his eternal Son, the expression of his eternal love, should become the saviour of the world by taking Israel's role on himself and dying, as Israel, the Servant of the Lord, for the sin of the world. This is the sequence of thought in the great hymn of Philippians 2:5-11. This is the heart of the Biblical Gospel: this is the way in which the overarching purpose of God in history illuminates every aspect of the rest of scripture, and becomes the context in which the whole saving truth, incarnation and atonement alike, is to be understood.

4.   Gospel and Church

We have now – to return to our original illustration – laid the explosive charge at the centre of the log-jam. These next three sections will indicate, in a more exploratory and tentative fashion, the effect that it may be expected to have on our understanding of the Church, the Bible and the Ministry. We begin by asking: what are the *ecclesiological implications* of the biblical Gospel we have set out above?

4.1.   *Historical and Visible*

Just as Jesus of Nazareth remains human – becomes, indeed, more fully what God always intended man to be – in the resurrection, so the people of God become a more fully human and hence historical community in the transformation (from Israel 'according to the flesh' to the world-wide church) which Jesus' death and resurrection effect. This highlights a weakness in traditional evangelical thinking. With notable exceptions, evangelicals have been weak in exploring the significance of Jesus' humanity, sometimes contenting themselves with a use of the incarnation as an argument for involvement in the world: and exactly the same weakness is apparent in much evangelical ecclesiology, which has failed to take seriously the nature of the church as the historical and visible people of God. Both errors are a form of Docetism (see p. 86 above). The effects have been that theological emphases have been retained as much because tradition insists on them as because they have been thought through. (It is, granted, far better to continue with a view of (e.g.) mission which blindly insists on certain biblical texts and a traditional interpretation of them than to abandon them pending fuller theological investigation: nevertheless such investigation would have undergirded the position with new strength and given it new urgency.) To continue with that example, it is in worldwide mission (with its corollaries of obedience and suffering) that the church lives as the historical and visible people of God. Mission does not consist in the church making forays into the enemy territory of space and time to take captives and bring them back to an invisible and timeless realm. Biblical theology centres on a flesh-and-blood Saviour and a flesh-and-blood community. It is precisely within Protestantism of an anti-incarnational stamp that the necessity for worldwide mission has recently been strongly denied: compare the work of John Hick. History is not an accident, a blunder on God's part. It needs redeeming, and the gospel does redeem it. God has not designed the gospel to spread in an historical vacuum. And this means that not only the preaching of the word, but also baptism and the Lord's Supper, are all-important as historical and visible marks of the church: see below, section 6 (page 107).

At the same time, we cannot simply affirm the historical nature of the church as though historical and visible continuity guaranteed grace. On the contrary. The church lives true to itself when she obeys the call to take up the cross. If that means self-denial at a personal level, at a corporate level it will mean that tradition and custom and fashionable ideas are all to be laid on the altar before God to he sacrificed if he so will. If the church is, in Charles Gore's favourite phrase, an extension of the incarnation, it is constantly required to recognise both the differences between itself and its Lord's incarnation (he was perfect, unique, the only saviour: the church is the sinful object of that salvation) and also the corollaries of that incarnation: he was found in fashion as a man and became obedient unto death, even the death of the cross. The call to bear the cross summons the historical and visible people of God to share the sufferings of Christ (notice how Colossians 1:24 ff. directly follows vv. 9-23), to share the sorrows and pains of the world which he came to be identified with and so to save. The visible Body of Christ is to be recognised, as its Master, by the mark of the nails. And, if that is the outward form of cross-bearing, the inward form, as suggested a moment ago, is a common life lived under judgment as well as salvation – a life in which the Word challenges, rebukes and corrects. Paul had to rebuke Peter at Antioch (Galatians 2): Peter pronounced God's judgment on Ananias and Sapphira shortly after Pentecost (Acts 5). A visible church that is not continually reforming itself under the word of God calls its very existence into question. The continuity of the church is itself at risk unless the discontinuity of continual reformation is also present. A church that seeks merely to save its life, merely to preserve itself for posterity, will lose it.

Within this context, the famous Pauline picture of the church as the 'Body of Christ' can be seen not merely as a way of encouraging 'every-member ministry' or mutual interdependence – though to be sure it does that – but as a means of emphasizing the nature of the church as the historical people of the Messiah. The background to the idea is not to be found in Stoic or other pagan imagery, as many have suggested, but in Old Testament ideas connected with *God* and his people on the one hand, and the *king* and his people on the other. Thus (e.g.) in Ephesians 5:25-32 the church as Christ's body is to be understood on the analogy of the 'one flesh' of marriage (cf. Genesis 2:23): the church is Christ's bride, just as Israel was seen in the Old Testament as God's bride. Again, the contexts of 1 Corinthians 10-12 and Romans 12 suggest the full meaning of 'Messiah', i.e. the anointed king of Israel, who sums up his people in himself, as in 2 Samuel 5:1 ff., where David is anointed because the tribes of Israel claim him as their 'bone and flesh'. Paul has taken this frequent Old Testament idea and transformed it in the light of the cross and resurrection: the Messiah's people are not now his *fleshly* relations, but those now identified with his risen *body*. Both ideas – man and wife, and the risen representative Lord – come together in the difficult passage 1 Corinthians 6:12-20. (I have set out the argument of this paragraph more fully in a forthcoming work.)

4.2. *Embodiment of the Gospel*

The church thus *embodies* the gospel of the death and resurrection of Jesus Christ. This is not merely to say that the church must live up to its own standards, or that it should be a large-scale visual aid of the truths it propounds, as though the gospel were still primary and the church secondary. While it is true that details of church polity etc. are ultimately secondary matters, the church itself is a primary matter, inseparable from the gospel itself, the message about Jesus Christ which can only be understood in the context of the church from Abraham to the present day and on to the Second Coming. The church is *part* of the Gospel: one component of the message of salvation is that in Jesus Christ God has created, is creating and will create 'a people for his own possession'. The church is not something tacked on at the end of the gospel as in much old dogmatic theology and much modern evangelical misunderstanding. If the gospel is wrenched out of the context of the people of God, it will not resonate with all its true overtones: that is, it cannot be properly understood except as the climax of Israel's history and the foundation of the church.

It is for this reason – to unpack all this a little – that we can claim that the Church of England, in its history and formularies, offers to the Evangelical a communion which, in theory at least, takes seriously just those aspects of ecclesiology which the gospel demands. The anglican church claims to be a 'Catholic' church in the full meaning of that word: it believes firmly in the historical nature of the church, highlighted particularly in its ministry and sacraments: it professes to be *ecclesia semper reformanda*, as must any church which, like Jesus and the apostles, puts the Bible at the centre of its life. As we should expect, it is not a perfect church: but it has written into its constitution just those checks and balances – submission of all things to scripture, and commitment within that to order and continuity – which indicate that the Gospel of Jesus Christ is, in theory at least, being lived out. When 'Evangelicals' look at the anglican communion, they do not need to destroy it and build something else, or to get out and go elsewhere. They need to help the church to become more truly itself – just as the anglican church provides a context within which evangelicals, committed by the biblical gospel to membership in the historical church, can live out that corporate. and sacramental life which is itself part of the gospel. We will return to this point in our conclusion.

4.3. Towards a Catholic Protestantism (or vice versa)

These suggestions point towards the daunting task of claiming that there may be more to the Gospel than Protestantism has usually seen or at least appropriated. Speaking very broadly, 'Catholic' Christians have tended to emphasize world-affirming views – the historical continuity of the church, the essential goodness of humanity, the value of the created order etc. – while 'Protestant' Christians have tended to emphasize a world-denying position – the church needs always to be purged and reformed under the word, history is a dangerous realm (see the next section), and 'the world lies in the power of the evil one'. There are notable exceptions on both sides, and indeed reactions against the prevailing mood within each side (ascetic tendencies within Catholicism, and world-affirming tendencies within Reformed theology): but the broad outline fits the case and actually determines a good deal of the theological positions which individuals and whole groups take up. 'Catholics' are anxious to safeguard what they see as the goodness of creation, and the positive nature of God's purposes for man and the world, against what they see as Protestant iconoclasm, individualism, anti-clericalism and ultimately man-centred rationalism. And there have been many theologians in the last four hundred years, particularly in the 'Protestant' theology which owes as much to the Enlightenment as to Luther, in which these Catholic fears appear to be justified. Evangelicalism is not immune to this danger. But equally well, Protestant fears – of a church that stifles the word, and preaches 'pipeline' grace and 'magic' sacraments, of a religion of works and man-centred clericalism – have been justified in many cases and areas. Some of the Evangelicals who replied to the CEEC questionnaire have obviously spent years of ministry fighting just this sort of 'Catholic' theology and practice at a local level.

But ultimately this spectrum of opinion is misleading. Apart from anything else, it flattens issues out, so that evangelicals feel compelled to deny the world in order to avoid underwriting it, and Catholics feel compelled to overstate the significance of sacraments (etc.) in order to avoid undercutting them altogether. It is this simplistic polarization which caused several evangelicals to vote in favour of the ordination of women in the recent debates, lest by opposing it they should seem to espouse that 'high' view of ordination which the leading opponents were putting forward as their main argument. Protestant principles appeared to dictate that one should stand firm against apparent clericalism, in the belief that one was thereby striking a blow for the gospel, for the principle that Christ alone (and not the parson) is the mediator between God and men, and that men and women are saved on the same terms. We will return to this below. For the moment we note that the 'spectrum' which places Catholics and Protestants at poles apart from one another is potentially misleading: for as soon as we ask 'what is it that you are attempting to safeguard', both sides (at any rate, those who know their onions) will reply 'genuine, biblical, God-centred Christianity'. It is a curious fact, which first came to the notice of many people with the publication of *Growing Into Union*, that 'Catholics' and 'Protestants' have each traditionally suspected the other of Pelagianism.

It is therefore important to distinguish between the biblical insights of Catholicism and Protestantism and the purely polemical positions which either side has felt obliged to construct, over and above biblical evidence, to safeguard those insights from attack. And, having made that distinction, it is important to bring together the biblical insights of each side within a larger framework that will do justice to each. This enormous task, I believe, is of considerable urgency for the church, though the present essay can do no more than point in a few directions in which the task might be accomplished.

At the same time, we will want to insist that some positions taken up not for polemical but for devotional or dogmatic reasons are simply wrong; examples might include Mariolatry or 'Benediction' on the Catholic side and the doctrinaire insistence on the *Textus Receptus* and the Authorized Version which is becoming common on the Protestant side. In other words, we must work towards a framework of thought within which the strong points of both sides can be included and from which the weak points – symptoms that understanding has been distorted, or has not been complete – can be excluded. It will no longer do to work with the assumption that Protestant principles by themselves – or Catholic ones, for that matter! – will automatically safeguard the gospel. We cannot assume, as some do today, that our problems are an exact 'action replay' of the sixteenth century, calling simply for a few modern Luthers to stop the Pope and all his works. On the contrary, to become more 'Protestant' may in fact mean becoming more man-centred, not less, as we shall see presently. We must beware too of the non-theological reasons often underlying polemical positions. Rome is often seen by Englishmen as the foreign invader, now happily repulsed but always threatening to return: and Catholics often base their picture of Protestants on American 'hot-gospellers' and Ian Paisley.

Our earlier remarks about nature and grace suggest that the church must be marked both by historical continuity and by a readiness to submit to God's judgment, to admit error, to sit under the Word and learn fresh truth from it. This is, of course, a programme for large-scale ecumenical thought and action: for our present purposes we note that it is also a call for evangelical Anglicans to rethink traditional attitudes about the church, and bring them more into line with the Bible and the Gospel.

5. *The Setting of Scripture*

To call for the church to sit under the Word implies a particular view of the Bible: and this raises several questions which are themselves near the heart of the so-called 'identity problem'. Many of the replies to the CEEC questionnaire focussed on Scripture as a major area of concern: and, though the problems raised here are wider than Anglicanism, something useful may briefly be said. A good many puzzled evangelicals tend to say in a crisis 'it all depends on whether you accept Scripture as the ultimate norm', and of course they are right. Several of the problems facing the church at present would look very different if everybody took the evangelical view of the Bible – which, Evangelicals maintain, is the Bible's view of itself. Equally, though, there are many problems which are not, apparently, brought nearer to a solution on this basis. There are no texts to guide us through Schemes of Unity between different denominations: and half the problem about the Ordination of Woman is precisely how to interpret and apply those passages which some think are germane to the issue. Like it or not, the question of 'hermeneutics' is here to stay.

The framework of thought we have suggested, however, indicates that we may in the past have made a false polarization in the problem of biblical interpretation. Evangelicals have rightly insisted that the Bible, not the church, is the final court of appeal: but at a popular level this has often been taken to mean that Bible and church are exclusive alternatives. The Bible itself warns against this. Scripture is not a detached entity, standing free to one side of the life and thought of God's people. It does not merely comment from a distance, as it were, on the history of God's dealings with his people, or convey theological information as though in a vacuum. The Bible is it self part of the covenant: its words are the words of obedient men who, through that Spirit-inspired obedience, freely write the words which bring God's order to the chaos of the world. The Bible is part of the process whereby God's Spirit restores man, and Israel, in Jesus Christ: and it both exemplifies this in the process of its inspiration (humanity is not turned into a typewriter) and helps to bring this about in the church by taking up the minds and the hearts of God's people so that they gladly and freely come to think the way God thinks. The necessity of 'hermeneutics' is God's way of ensuring, via his gift of historical and cultural change, that every generation has to grow up to full understanding for itself, cannot simply mouth sound language inherited from before, has to read the Bible for itself in order to retain a living faith which matches that of its forefathers. Precisely because the Bible is God's word in human words, its role within the covenant plan is a dynamic, not a static one.

But this necessarily means that the Bible is not a mere collection of 'timeless truths'. On the contrary, the Bible is written out of highly individual human contexts. One sometimes hears evangelicals talking and debating as if certain passages were 'culturally conditioned' and *therefore dispensible*: a good deal of evangelical confusion, not least on ethical questions, springs from this misunderstanding. But all the Bible is 'culturally conditioned' – not only the bits about ethical problems but also the great doctrinal passages and the well-loved prophecies and promises. This in no way prevents us from continuing to use the Bible as our norm and standard. But looking for 'timeless truths' is in fact part of an attempt to distil ideas and principles out of their original contexts and reapplying them in the present day – analogous, in fact, to the allegorical method and to Bultmann's demythologization. It is itself a hermeneutical method, not usually recognised as such because it is so engrained in evangelical habits (others do it too, of course), but dangerously open to arbitrary and misleading operation. All such methods tend to imply that life would be much easier if there were no such thing as historical change and consequent cultural distance, as though God had somehow blundered in giving us a Bible which is so difficult to understand and interpret. This problem, in fact, lies for many at the heart of the current Identity Problem: many who have been used to reading Scripture in a particular way feel challenged and threatened when others insist on interpreting well-known passages in fresh ways, against their original background and context, and they think that those who suggest this are therefore 'going soft on scripture'. This is not helped by the presence within evangelicalism of some who are using the 'culturally conditioned' argument (see above) in order to evade what seems to others very direct and unequivocal teaching on some topic or other. But the 'timeless truth' position is itself not taking the Bible seriously. It implies that God has given us the wrong sort of book, and that we must somehow turn it into the right kind.

But if we recognize the true ecclesiological dimension of the gospel – if we see the church as the historical covenant community – this problem becomes quite different. The process of history which has distanced us from the biblical period is no peculiar accident, no blunder on God's part. On the contrary, history is the sphere of God's sovereign providential rule. The problem of hermeneutics is a peculiarly *Protestant* problem: to recognize the importance of the historical church poses the question quite differently. The trouble seems to be that evangelicals, like Protestants in general, have been so concerned not to allow 'Tradition' a place *above* Scripture or alongside it that we have failed to give it its rightful place *beneath* Scripture. God, who inspired scripture in the first place by his Spirit, continues to guide the church by that same Spirit to reform itself and its thinking under the word, and, more, to take captive the muddled secular thinking of the world and bring it into captivity to the gospel. This process – often partial, often misguided, but nevertheless constituting real advances and establishing a corpus of insights themselves dependent upon, and to be checked against, scripture, is the God-given context in which the church needs and reads the Bible. The Bible was produced in the context of the covenant community: the tradition of the church consists in its attempts, down the ages, to read the Bible in this context: and the Bible speaks today in the same covenant context, which now includes that tradition.

In fact, we *can* only read the Bible in this way. We cannot escape from the fact that we all come to scripture with questions and ideas which come to us from our tradition. Every sermon we preach or hear hands on a tradition of interpretation. This is not something to be ashamed of. The Holy Spirit did not stop work when the last book of the New Testament was written, but has been at work ever since to help the church to understand the word. We all in fact do read the Bible in the context of our traditions, and evangelicals who fail to realise this are therefore peculiarly in danger of failing to re-check their traditions in the light of scripture, and of hearing the voice of the tradition imagining it to be the voice of the Word itself. What I am suggesting is that we should not only recognize that this *in fact* happens, but also that God intends that it should happen. Only if we are living in the context of the covenant community – only if we are sharing in the sacraments, in the historical life of the people of God – can the Bible really be *our* book. This *in no way* sets up the church, or tradition, as the final authority over against Scripture, because it is precisely the task of the church to be constantly re-evaluating this tradition in the light of scripture. (For all this, compare *Growing Into Union* p. 37.) We must not put the cart before the horse, but nor may we suggest that the cart doesn't matter provided we've got the horse. Our job is to be in the cart, pulled by the horse: to live with the tradition of the whole church, constantly submitting it for checking, improvement, correction and elaboration to the written word of God.

6.   The Marks of the Church

6.1.   *Ministry and Sacraments*

If the church is to learn from the word, the New Testament view of how this is to happen is through the teaching ministry which God gives to individuals within the people of God. In fact, though in this section we can do no more than outline certain corollaries from what has been said so far, we can claim that, under the Holy Spirit, 'ministry' is God's means of enabling the church to *be* the church. If the church is to be marked out, as the reformers insisted, as the place where the word is preached, the sacraments administered and godly discipline imposed, this is to be done through God's call of some to exercise certain roles as ministers – i.e. servants – of the people of God. God characteristically works *through* people, by the Spirit – not 'direct', in a way which by-passes all other agencies.

'Ministry' is a word with multiple connotations. It seems clear from various passages (1 Corinthians 12 is the shining example) that *every* member of the Body of Christ has some 'ministry', some service which he or she is to offer to the church as a whole. It is often remarked that there should be no comma in Ephesians 4:12 between the phrases 'for the equipment of the saints' and 'for the work of ministry': every 'saint', i.e. every Christian, has a ministry, and it is the role of specialized 'ministries' to equip all God's people for their own tasks. We will return to this presently.

But Ephesians 4:11 ff. makes it quite clear that some members of the church are to be set aside as evangelists, teachers, etc. (It is not our purpose here to describe the offices in full, but only to note the principles.) God gives these ministries to his church to enable the church to *be* the church. Evangelists act as the spearhead of the church's missionary work which as we have seen is an essential mark of her present historical existence. Pastors and teachers enable the church to live (corporately, individually, doctrinally and ethically) under the word of God. Apostles and prophets (this is of course controversial, but cf. Ephesians 2:20) are part of the original historical foundation of the people of God, the new community into which Israel has been transformed. And all the offices together are intended (Ephesians 4:12b-16) to work together towards the *unity* of the 'one body' (cf. vv. 3-6).

Paul explicitly connects baptism with this unity: there is one baptism, even as there is one Lord and one faith (Ephesians 4:5). In addition, he regards the Lord's Supper as a means and mark of unity, so that disunity at the Supper is a great scandal (1 Corinthians 11:17 ff.). In the light of this it is appropriate – to put it for the moment no higher – if the one who baptizes, and who 'presides' (if that word may be used without dangerous overtones) at the Supper is the one in whose *office* the church can see the mark of visible unity with other contemporary congregations and with the great church that has existed since Abraham and will exist until all its members share the glory of its Lord. The two sacraments mark out the historical and visible church: it is totally fitting if they are administered by those commissioned to act as historical and visible representatives of that church. Insofar as the present call for lay 'celebration' is motivated by an anti-clericalism that secretly wishes to level out all Christians as though Ephesians 4 and 1 Corinthians 12 were not there, it is to be resisted: though it is of course true that the phrase 'pastoral necessity' is often invoked as an extra argument. (While this is clear in the case of baptism – and was even clearer when the fate of unbaptized infants was viewed more pessimistically than it was by the Reformers – it remains a moot point whether it is ever 'pastorally necessary' for an unauthorized person to administer Communion; this, while going through the motions of the Sacrament of unity, denies ontologically its unity with the rest of the historical and visible church.)

At the very point (baptism and the supper) where the historical continuity of the people of God is most marked, the cross is also central (Romans 6:2. ff., 1 Corinthians 11:23. ff). Whereas circumcision had pointed back to the Patriarch, and the Passover to the national liberation at the Exodus, the Christian sacraments, which like those of the old covenant still mark out God's people within history, point even as they do so to the events which give that community its particular character. The sacraments are not just 'means of grace' if by that is meant 'ways in which the individual Christian, or even the individual congregation, may know and love God more and serve him better'. They are 'means of grace' also in the sense that in and through baptism the church's history, and the world's history, as well as the history of the individual concerned, really is being caught up into the saving purposes of God, and that in and through the regular celebration of the Lord's Supper the worldwide historical people of God is being marked out, as a line of cairns show the mountaineer where the true path to the summit may be found. As often as you eat this bread and drink this cup, you show forth the Lord's death until he comes. If we call the sacraments 'visible words', it is not because they are simply visual aids, but because, like the Word of God itself, they bring into order and coherence the history of the church and the world. They truly say 'here is the people of God', and they explain who and what that people is: that is, they provide the faithful with assurance that they are indeed members of that family, and at the same time demonstrate to the world that salvation is to be found in belonging to the historical people constituted through the death and resurrection of Jesus Christ, the object of Christian faith.

We cannot simply go through the motions of using water, bread and wine and hope that we will thus attain salvation. The only context in which these actions have saving significance is that of obedient faith, which is of course itself based on the cross and resurrection. It cannot be too strongly emphasized that this 'effectual sign' view of the sacraments (see *Growing Into Union* p.54 ff., Packer *Evangelical Anglican Identity* p. 2) is not 'magic'. It is a matter of history: the actual history of the people concerned is now radically different. But nor can we simply regard the sacraments as 'bare signs': they are effectual signs, because they are part of a God-given order which is in process of being realized, albeit (at the moment) visible only to the eye of faith. The necessity for faith for the appropriation of the sacraments is therefore subtly different from the usual conception. Most Protestants would say that, without faith, nothing 'happens': and the corollary is, for instance, that the eating and drinking', which are really 'spiritual', can be done just as well by faith without coming to the physical table and receiving the physical elements. But this misses the point, as is clear from 1 Corinthians 11:29-32. It elevates the exceptional case (of those who are physically unable to receive the sacrament) into a norm. The actions, and the elements, *are* the thing itself. Christianity is not divorced from history and the physical world. If one wants assurance that one belongs to the people of God, the outward signs are what God offers. But such assurance *is* faith, because only faith, looking at the water of baptism or the token meal of the supper, can perceive that the former initiates, and the latter nourishes, the true historical and eschatological life of the people of the crucified and risen Jesus Christ. Faith 'hears' the 'word' which is made visible precisely in the sacraments, *and which cannot normally be replaced or substituted for by anything else* (though preaching is of course essential for the congregation to grasp the meaning: see above). If the sacraments are ignored or played down; if they are constantly being apologized for, as in some evangelical parishes; if church life is so organized that Christians are denied the chance to develop a healthy appreciation of them, for instance by holding Communion services at different times every week of the month ('pastorally necessary' sometimes maybe, but often done for (inadequate) reasons of tradition and theology); true Christian faith is denied part of the authentic context within which it may flourish.

6.2. *Office and Function*

The same context, of the historical, visible and sacramental people of God (which is not something apart from the Gospel, but is as we have seen combined with the nature of the evangelical gospel itself) provides the means whereby we can advance also in the vexed area of the church's ministry. Many are saying today that the 'one-man band' style of ministry is outmoded, unBiblical, inefficient and unevangelical. I agree. But there is no consensus as to what theology of ministry should underlie attempts to reform our present structures, and such attempts are therefore themselves confused. Should we scrap all division between clergy and laity? What does the great Reformation slogan 'Priesthood of all believers' mean today? Some apparently think (to judge from recent experience as well as from the answers to the CEEC questionnaire) that the clergy-laity division is completely wrong (it was only because of strong protests that the Nottingham Statement did not describe it as 'disastrous'). We find ordained men taking services in lounge suits (albeit, in one recent televised service, flanked by a robed choir!). We find ordained men who, instead of reading the carefully-worded absolution set in the Book of Common Prayer, opt instead for the Collect for the twenty-first Sunday after Trinity as if they were laymen or deacons, and who carefully say 'us' instead of 'you' when giving a blessing at the end of the service. What are we to make of all this?

I believe that this whole situation represents muddled thinking. Some Evangelicals, afraid of crypto-Romanism, have opted instead for an anti-clericalism which owes more to the slightly trendy, democratizing Spirit of the Age than it does to Biblical principles. Others are genuinely trying to reverse a trend of clerical domination, or to involve laity to a greater extent in the church's life and worship. Some invoke the 'Body of Christ' picture as an argument for the 'equality' of all ministries. Many older anglican Evangelicals have been deeply affected by the principles and practice of the Plymouth Brethren.

But the danger now seems to be that, instead of the 'priesthood of all believers', we have ended up with the priesthood of no believers at all. The priesthood of all believers is an Old Testament idea, transferred from Israel in Exodus 19:6 to the church in 1 Peter 2:9 : and it never occurred to anyone – except Korah – to use the fact that the whole nation were 'priests' (in that sense) as an argument against the existence of a particular class of people who were 'priests' in a special sense. Likewise, Paul's use of the 'Body' metaphor in 1 Corinthians and Romans is specifically attacking the idea that all members of the church should have the *same* function. When discussing differing ministries, Paul clearly envisages that certain people will have roles which others will not have. This does not mean that some, let alone a majority, will have no ministry at all: each member will have his or her ministry. But this is no argument for anti-clericalism – unless, as I suspect has often happened, 'ministry' has still been understood as 'clerical ministry', so that 'every-member ministry' has come to mean 'every man a clergyman'. But it does nothing at all for the cause of 'the equipment of the saints for the work of ministry' for lay people to be invited to take over *someone else's* ministry: every-member ministry in Biblical terms means everyone having his or her *own* ministry. Properly understood, the Body of Christ is an egalitarian's nightmare: everybody is different, and God has so organized the differences that all fit together. It is sad to think of the confusions whereby twentieth-century egalitarianism has been mistaken for Protestantism, and this 'Protestantism' has been mistaken for the Gospel. God has appointed 'diverse orders' in his church – not (of course) to lord it over one another, nor to suggest (has anyone since mediaeval times ever really suggested this, or is it just a caricature?) that one category of people is more 'saved' or more 'justified' than others – but to serve one another in complementary, not identical, ways. The discovery of the importance of lay ministry, in which the charismatic movement has played a significant part, is no argument for the abolition of clerical ministry, but makes it all the more necessary, if 'decency' and 'order' are to be maintained, as Paul insists in 1 Corinthians 14. The New Testament clearly envisages different levels of authority within the people of God (e.g. Hebrews 13:17, 24).

The various functions which the ordained man is to perform are therefore not evidence that he has a 'merely functional' ministry. In virtue of his ordination, in which God and the church have set him aside for this purpose, the minister is different, not magically (as 'pipeline' grace would have it) but historically: like the baptized person, he leaves church a different person from what he was before. He has been publicly entrusted with tasks to perform and has publicly promised to perform them and to live the appropriate sort of life. He cannot now behave as if all this were not true without living a lie. He holds an *office* within the church, not in virtue of who he is personally (though life and character should match the dignity of the office), but in virtue of the ministry entrusted to him. That is, though the distinction between the uniform and the wearer should not obtrude, it is always present and should sometimes be called upon to avoid misunderstandings. In particular, the person who officiates at a service should *not* do so 'because' he is a man of deep spirituality or wisdom, though it is appropriate if he is in fact that. Any suggestion to the contrary, any idea that the officiant acts in virtue of his own character, is in fact a return to man-centred sacerdotalism, this time in a Protestant form, in which the man concerned comes between God and the people. The division between clergy and laity enables the church to worship, to hear the word, and to enjoy the sacraments, in a God-centred context rather than a man-centred one. The preacher or officiant will often be uncomfortably aware of the distance between his office and his personal piety: but this does not mean that the worship of the congregation he leads is not genuine. The Word preached is God's word, and the Communion table is the Lord's table, not that of any denomination or minister.

One feature of modern evangelicalism makes it all the

more necessary to stress this point. It is all very well for those with a natural flair for public speaking, chairing meetings, and so on, to see the ministry as merely the confirmation of certain functions which certain people find they can already fulfil. *Their* position is not in doubt. But there are plenty of people who are equally called by God, equally given teaching authority over the people of God, equally called to administer the sacraments, who are not cheerful extroverts, whose temperaments do not allow them to take to their duties by the light of nature, and who therefore would not dare exercise their ministry unless they were sure that this was something objective, given as a status by God, within which natural gifts could gradually develop under the power of the Holy Spirit. This is also the only way in which proper discipline can be exercised in the church, as evangelicals often insist that it should be. The exercise of discipline demands that the Bishop (or whoever) acts not as an individual but in virtue of the office and ministry entrusted to him, irrespective of his personal opinions and predilections. Protestants, of all people, should warm to the analogy between this view of ministry and justification by faith. My status as a Christian does not depend on how I feel, on what virtues or gifts or graces I may have, but simply on God's call and his declaration in Christ about me. In the same way, to stress the ontological character of the ordained ministry is to point away from what someone is in himself, and towards the call and historical action of God. That, not the self-confidence of the gifted leader, is the true basis of humble, Christ-like, God-centred ministry.

The same point could be made in relation to clerical dress, from dog-collars onwards. The greatest argument for a special 'uniform', particularly when doing things which are most appropriately done by an ordained person, is that this reminds officiant, preacher and congregation that the service is not being taken by a private individual, but by the one who is the appointed representative of God' s authority over his people, charged with a teaching ministry. He also forms the historical and visible link between this congregation and the worldwide historical church. Ideally, putting on 'robes' (I hold no brief for any particular outfits, except to say that simplicity would be both sufficient and appropriate) should not make the officiant give himself airs: it should make him realise that he does what he is about to do not as John Smith, the up-and-coming young preacher, the beloved pastor of these dear people, the respected thinker or Synodsman, but as a servant, set aside despite his total unworthiness for the humbling and sometimes crushing task of the ministry. If he realises that, he will be all the better a preacher and a pastor for it. If you put the office and status first (who the minister *is*, in virtue of his ordination), function (what he is to *do*) will follow, always assuming that a man is truly called and submits to the Word of God. Elevate function to the supreme place, even for the best of motives, and all will ultimately disappear in a man-centred ministry, whether it is a one-man band or an every-member orchestra.

One curious thing about the position towards which I am arguing is that, though it flies in the face of much contemporary evangelical thinking, it bears a close resemblance to the theology of the great mainline reformers. One of the biggest difficulties evangelicals face as they debate unity schemes, the ordination of women, or tricky ethical questions is that many of them are shadow-boxing, fighting battles at second hand, half-defending half-remembered positions they fear are in danger, or half-attacking half-remembered ideas they fear are leading the church astray. But theology done in a fog like that is not helpful: it isn't even fun. We need to see more clearly, as the reformers did, what we are all talking about. The reformers rejected, of course, all forms of ecclesiastical 'magic' ('pipeline grace', transubstantiation, etc.), as we have done: but at the same time they refused to water down the church to a mere agglomeration of like-minded Christians, or the ministry to the mere exercise of different functions, or the sacraments to mere visual aids. We are therefore in line neither with the Bible, nor the Gospel, nor the mainline reformers, if we think that the best defence of evangelicalism – or even of the Gospel! – is simply to lower the churchmanship another peg or two. God's truth is more subtle and exciting than that. Because we are Bible people and Gospel people, we are compelled also to be *Church* people. Insofar as the Anglican church exhibits those features of ecclesiology we have sought to expound, being anglican *Evangelicals* means that we must also be evangelical *Anglicans.*

7. *Evangelical, Anglican ... and Confused?*

In writing as I have, I have been aware of one great need and one great danger. The need, which is not of course satisfied by the present study, is for the Biblical Gospel to be rethought creatively by every generation of Christians, not to undercut what we already know (though we too need to be *semper reformanda)* but to develop and mature our understanding of it. God has yet more light – much more – to break out of his holy word. When we find ourselves in an Identity Problem perhaps the most appropriate thing to do is to pray, and work, for that fresh light: to read the Bible as a new book with new things to say - which will at the same time be to go back to its original meaning, to re-emphasize old truths, basic certainties, but often with delicate nuances and emphases we had missed because we had ignored them, which will challenge us to reform ourselves afresh, as we traditionally insist that every one else should do.

The danger, to which Dr. Packer alludes (page 45 f. above), is that we should apparently add to the Gospel and so in fact subtract from it. I hope and believe that the above exposition has not done this, but has rather drawn out of the Gospel essential features which were there all along. As far as I can see, the great Gospel emphases – Christ alone, faith alone, Scripture alone and grace alone – are enhanced, not undercut, by the theology of God's work in and through man and history which I have tried to expound. Though I have tried to add to contemporary evangelical understanding of the gospel, I have no desire whatever to add to the all-sufficient gospel itself.

If I thought that our present Identity Problems were the result of creative rethinking of theology in the light of Scripture, I would regard it as a very healthy sign. But I am not sure whether this is the case. I believe, in fact, that our present Problem is occurring at a prior stage. It has come about because we have recently been faced with a whole range of issues for which our tradition has no ready-made answers. We have come out of our ghettoes, elected serried ranks into synods, sat on committees, and have found that the slogans and principles which kept our spirits up when we were a tiny minority have less to say now than they used to. We have grown up with the sense that we were called to evangelicalize the Anglican communion: and now, on taking that communion seriously, we find it in no way obvious how that process should be carried out.

What I have suggested in this essay is that this is precisely the sort of situation through which God leads his people to fresh explorations of his truth. If this means spending more time in prayer ard meditation, more time at the desk reading, praying, trying out ideas in notebooks, more time in pastoral counselling and spiritual direction, and less time in committees, discussions and paperwork, that will be an excellent thing.

It is all too easy these days for a young evangelical clergyman to spend the best hours of the week (when he could and should be thinking and praying his way not only towards his next sermon and his forthcoming pastoral ministry but also towards making the church and himself more biblical in every way) in activities which, in the long term, will not make him or the church more biblical or more Christ-like. If we really believe in every-member ministry, let those who are called to do so delegate all that can be delegated, and come with uncluttered minds to the fresh study of God's word and of the great tradition of Christian writing in which we stand. I have been suggesting certain lines of thought which, though no doubt strange to some evangelicals, seem to me to arise within the biblical gospel itself, and which demand our attention if we are to grow in our understanding to meet the challenges of a new day.

What has all this done to our Identity Problem? I suggest that, in terms of the circles of identity with which we began this paper, it has enlarged the right hand circle so as to take in more of the left hand one.

Instead of the Idealistic Constitutionalists, who regard

Anglicanism as a sub-class of Evangelicalism

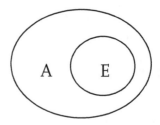

and the Contemporary Realists, who live in the shaded area where the two circles overlap

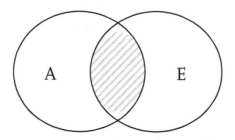

I suggest that the evangelical gospel itself is a larger thing, emphasizing of its own accord those doctrines of Word, Sacrament and Ministry which have often been associated with the Anglican heritage but not so often with 'Evangelicalism'. This has the effect of enlarging the right-hand circle so as to include far more actual Anglican theology than is usually thought:

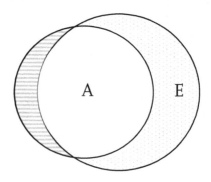

There will still remain some features (in the lined area) which cannot be squared with the gospel (Mariolatry, recurrent liberalism, etc.): and we may well feel that Anglicanism has still some lessons to learn from Evangelicalism (the dotted area: e.g. a full understanding of the cross). But we will be in a position to appeal to our fellow-Anglicans, with some hope of credibility, that, as we take them seriously and have learnt in fellowship with them truths we might otherwise have forgotten, so they should look again and see if in our theology they may not find fresh ideas from Scripture, ignored before because they were presented unpalatably or misleadingly, but now set free to enrich the whole church.

Our aim will then be to encourage our fellow-Anglicans to join us in a continual reformation, so as to grow into the full truth of Bible, Gospel and Church, in such a way that the Anglican circle in the diagram can itself be enlarged and recentred, with the aim of the two circles becoming concentric and in fact identical. (When a renewed and reformed evangelical movement can be seen to have this effect on Anglicanism, there will be less and less reason for lasting division between Anglicans and the Free Churches). This aim is, of course, idealistic. I said at the outset that there were fresh peaks waiting to be conquered. Frankly, it is difficult to see the process taking less than a generation or two at the very least. But part of our Identity Problem has been a loss of vision, an uncertainty about methods and presuppositions, about intermediate aims and goals, and consequently about strategy and tactics.

To that Identity Problem (have we perhaps re-identified it as a Confusion?) we return in conclusion. We have suggested that the way forward is an enlarged vision of the biblical gospel itself; and we have hinted at certain ways in which that dynamic gospel, applied like an explosive charge to the log-jam of contemporary debate, might be expected to shift the logs and get them moving again. The Bible is to be seen as the human and divine book which is to be read and interpreted within the context of, and as the rule of life for, the historical and visible church. Allegiance to the visible church, not just to inter-denominational parties and structures, matters as being ultimately a part of the gospel itself.

Liturgical revision – or rather, what we do with our new liturgy now we've got it – must be thought out in the light not of old slogans but fresh biblical and sacramental thinking. Above all, evangelical traditions must be subjected to proper biblical scrutiny (not merely a search for proof-texts): some will emerge triumphantly, others will need to be jettisoned. If we are all committed to this task – and the present author has actually changed his mind on one or two relevant issues in the course of writing this paper – there is hope that, in love and patience with each other, we may be able to move into the future with fewer worries about our own identity and more eagerness to play our full part within the whole saving purposes of God. I am suggesting that we explore together the full meaning of being Gospel people, Bible people and Church people, in the certain knowledge that this will make us better evangelicals and better Anglicans, because better Christians. Evangelical Anglicanism has reached a new and disturbing stage in its history. We need a new vision if we are to be true to God and to ourselves in the days to come.

LATIMER STUDIES 10

A Kind of Noah's Ark? The Anglican Commitment to Comprehensiveness

by J. I. Packer

first published 1981

Latimer Study 10 Contents

Foreword

Dear Joe,

Your question calls for more than I can put in a letter, so I have written this small book on it. Don't be embarrassed; Luther wrote a book on prayer specially for Peter his barber (a gem, incidentally), so why shouldn't I write a book on being an Anglican specially for you? If there's sense in it others beside you will get the benefit, and if it turns out like Eccles in the old Goon Show ('I don't say much, but what I say – don't make sense') you won't be held responsible.

I know you're not yet sure whether to offer for ordination, and you mustn't think that by this grand gesture I'm trying to put pressure on you. If God wants you in the ordained ministry he'll put on all the pressure that's needed, and you'll find yourself having to say, in the words of the great Spike Milligan walking backwards for Christmas (remember?), 'it's the only thing for me.' But thinking chaps like you are needed in the Anglican ministry, and I don't want needless stumbling-blocks to lie in their way.

You asked me how an evangelical who takes seriously his stewardship of revealed truth can ever with a good conscience take office in the Church of England when it is such a doctrinal Noah's ark, parading a comprehensiveness under which, as it seems, literally anything goes. That's an important question, and a fair one, since I am in fact a clergyman, and you are by no means the only person to put it to me, and I'd like the world to have my answer.

Whether I take my stewardship of revealed truth seriously enough others must decide, but I can say this: For a generation now I have had close links with Free Church evangelicals who spared no effort to show me that as an Anglican I am in a false position. I think I know their arguments pretty well by now. Yet though Anglican doctrinal pluralism brings as much distress today as ever it did, I was never so sure that as an Anglican I'm where I should be, and where many others should be too. I want to share the lines of thought that brought me here. So please read on.

Sincerely

JIM PACKER

1. Anglican Comprehensiveness – Virtue or Vice?

This essay is a companion piece to the first of the Latimer Studies which I wrote in 1978, entitled *The Evangelical Anglican Identity Problem*.[4] There I discussed what evangelicals in the Church of England stand for; here I ask what the Church of England itself stands for. I do so as an evangelical, and since this word means different things to different people I shall first spell out what I mean by it, so that no one will misunderstand where I am coming from in what follows.

1.1. *Evangelical Perspectives*

Anglicans who call themselves evangelicals, like those who claim to be Anglican (Anglo-) Catholics, see themselves as holding in trust for the rest of the church a heritage of truth and insight, perceptions of reality and duty, and traditions of stockpiled wisdom and spiritual experience, which form part of the wealth laid up in Christ for all, but which, partly through unawareness of true notions and partly through prepossession by false ones, not all up to now have been able to grasp. In my earlier study I noted as chief among the truths of which evangelicals are trustees:

> (1) the supremacy of Scripture as God-given instruction, a sufficient, self-interpreting guide in all matters of faith and action;
>
> (2) the majesty of Jesus Christ our sin-bearing divine Saviour and glorified King, by faith in whom we are justified;
>
> (3) the lordship of the Holy Spirit, giver of spiritual life by animating, assuring, empowering and transforming the saints;
>
> (4) the necessity of conversion, not as a stereotyped experience but as a regenerate condition, a state of faith in

---

[4] The Evangelical Anglican Identity Problem: An Analysis, Oxford: Latimer House, 1978, reprinted in this volume.

Christ evidenced by repentance and practical godliness;

(5) the priority of evangelism in the church's agenda;

(6) the fellowship of believers (the faith-full) as the essence of the church's life.[5]

Evangelicals stress that faith, like charity, must begin at home, in the sense that convertedness is first to seek because unconverted folk can neither know God's forgiveness and favour nor serve him or others as they should. Immature evangelicals have sometimes settled for a euphoric, man-centred pietism, concerned only with possessing and spreading the peace and joy of 'knowing Christ as my personal Saviour' (sadly, these precious words are nowadays a cant phrase), and never appreciating God's revealed concern for truth and righteousness in church and community. Maturer evangelicals, however, have always recognized that though personal conversion is the starting-point, Christians must learn a biblical God-centredness and seek after 'holiness to the Lord' in all departments of the church's worship, witness and work and in every activity and relationship of human life. Over the past four centuries in England this maturity has been most apparent when evangelicalism has been closest to its historical roots in Reformed (that is, Reformational, or, to use a word which would have distressed John Calvin, Calvinistic) theology.

'Evangelical' and 'Reformed' are not synonyms. Not all evangelicals, Anglican or other, would call themselves Reformed (some profess to be Lutheran, Wesleyan, Pentecostal or just nondescriptly biblicist); nor can all conservative Calvinists properly be called evangelicals (some are formalists in doctrine and devotion, some are institutionalists in pastoral care and strategy, and some are quietists wholly absorbed in monitoring the drama of God's life in their souls). But whenever evangelicalism is fuelled by teaching that reproduces the biblical theocentrism of Calvin's

---

[5] op. cit., pp 47 ff above. In the first chapter of *Knots Untied* (1877) J. C. Ryle defined evangelical religion in terms of the supremacy of Scripture, the sinfulness of man, the substitutionary atonement of Christ and the sanctifying work of the Spirit.

Institutes or the Anglican formularies or the later Westminster standards (drafted, be it said, mainly by Anglicans), all of which documents show the same balanced concern for personal faith, a pure church and a godly society, it manifests the mature breadth of which I am speaking.

At the turn of this century both Abraham Kuyper, architect of Reformed renewal in Holland, and G. K. Chesterton, the most potent Christian apologist in England (despite his sad misconception of Protestantism), were both saying from opposite sides of the fence that in construing Christianity the ultimate choice lies between Calvinism and Catholicism. Leaving aside the questions, which a well-informed person might want to press, as to whether the Reformed humanism of Kuyper was not more truly catholic, in the sense of comprehensively Christian, than Chesterton's romantic mediaevalism, and whether the backward-looking Catholicism of Chesterton was not really more sectarian, in the sense of unbiblically exclusive, than Kuyper's forward-looking Protestantism, we may agree with them at once. The Roman (Catholic) and Reformed (Calvinistic) really are the only traditions of Christian thought that have range and resources sufficient to become full-scale world-and-life-views – philosophies of life, in the old rich sense of that phrase, seeing all reality, activity and community steadily and whole, because it is all being looked at in relation to God's cosmic goals and plans and to the eternity (the world to come) to which it is all working up. And only when evangelicalism comes under Reformed tutelage (for substance, even if not by that name) does it successfully transcend the limitations of pietistic individualism and show itself as a viewpoint of biblical breadth.

Now the evangelical tradition of faith and life in the Church of England has been mostly fed by Reformed theology, and has characteristically been marked by deep concern, variously expressed, for godliness in both church and community, as well as in individuals and 'keen' groups. Think, for illustration, of the Reformers, and the Church Puritans who followed them; of the Church-oriented evangelicalism fostered by Simeon, Wilberforce, the Clapham fraternity and later by J. C. Ryle; and of the unacknowledged yet decided return of many Anglican evangelicals in our time to their Reformed roots, a return which has led to the strong wish expressed at the Keele and Nottingham congresses, that evangelicalism might be effective in reshaping and renewing church and nation today. The sort of pietism which withdraws from all constructive links with the church and the world save those with other evangelicals should not, therefore, be seen as an evangelical Anglican norm, any more than mediaeval relic-worship should be thought of as a Roman Catholic norm. The fact that some within evangelical circles and many outside them treat such pietism as the evangelical norm is sad and stultifying. To think of what is eccentric as ordinary, or decadent as standard, is grievously to misunderstand.

Certainly, this has not been a good century for Anglican evangelicals. Influence has shrunk and pietistic individualism has prevailed, leading many to suppose that nothing about the Church of England matters save that it is still the best boat to fish from. Despite the recent Reformed resurgence noticed above, it is clear that very many earnest Anglicans still think about their church in this way, and other things about it never bother them. But this shrugging off of concern as to what appearance the Church presents to the watching world, and how it nurtures its adherents, and how far its ways glorify God, is not the authentic evangelical attitude, nor is it the standpoint from which I write the present essay.

1.2. *Comprehensiveness – Unlimited?*

Anglican apologists often claim that one excellence of the Church of England is its comprehensiveness: that is, the way it finds room on its broad bosom for all sorts of Christians to lie comfortably side by side, amicably debating non-essentials on the basis of their happy agreement about basics. This (so it is urged) is one sign of the Church's catholic spirit, in other words its purpose of embracing the whole of Christian truth and its unwillingness to be a sect outlawing from its fellowship folk whom Christ accepts, just because they verbalise the faith eccentrically or differ from others on minor issues of faith and order.

The formula sounds good. It is obviously right in principle that a body like the Church of England, a nationwide federation of many thousand congregations in full communion with each other and seeking to embrace as many English Christians as possible while commending mainstream Christianity to all, should be as wide and tolerant in its embraces as the Christian revelation allows. It is obviously right that its creed should be restricted to the minimum necessary, and that on other matters its members be left free, in John Wesley's happy phrase, to 'think, and let think'. Historically, Anglicans have for the most part followed the judicious Richard Hooker in grounding the unity of the catholic visible church in its profession of the Christian fundamentals, namely the articles of the Apostles' and Nicene Creeds as interpreted by the Bible whose faith they intend to express. Evangelicals as a body go with this, though they insist that the forgiveness of sins in the creeds must be expounded in terms of justification by faith, as Hooker himself did.[6] And if all Anglicans were at one on the fundamentals, the comprehensiveness which allows for (e.g.) different notions of Christ's eucharistic presence, or different estimates of the importance of the historic Episcopal succession, or different opinions on the circumstances of Christ's return, or opposing views on the ethics of abortion and the propriety of making women presbyters, while not, perhaps, perfectly comfortable to live with, would present no problem of principle, to evangelicals or anyone else.

Sadly, however, the present-day reality of Anglican comprehensiveness is not like that. It is both more complex and more painful. There are two reasons for this. One is that since biblical criticism, in the sense of systematic study of the origins, composition, literary character and purpose of the biblical books as human documents, established itself in the Protestant world a century ago, many Anglicans have ceased to view Bible doctrine as God's revealed truth, and no longer let biblical thoughts determine

---

[6] See Hooker's *Learned Discourse of Justification, Works*, Oxford: OUP, 1875, II. 600 ff.

their thinking. Allowing Scripture great human authority as a primary witness to archetypal Christian experience, they deny it divine authority as instruction from heaven. So at every turn we find them distinguishing divine realities from New Testament ideas about them, and refusing to concede that they lose touch with the former by questioning the latter. But to those who believe that the Holy Spirit spoke by the prophets and their apostolic counterparts, making biblical testimony as truly God's utterance as were the words of the incarnate Son, and who take the fundamentals to be just what Scripture says they are, the claim to uphold those fundamentals while relativizing or recasting Scripture statements about them seems incoherent nonsense. Thus discussion of fundamentals falls into deep confusion, and the question whether there is essential agreement on what is essential to the essentials becomes problematical to the last degree.

Then, second, Broad Church liberals and radicals, spiritual heirs of the Latitudinarians of earlier times, proceeding on the basis of the view of Scripture outlined above, claim unlimited freedom to reconceive the Christian fundamentals. So today, for instance, brilliant University teachers like Don Cupitt, and Professors Maurice Wiles, Dennis Nineham and the late Geoffrey Lampe (to look no further), are Unitarian rather than trinitarian in their thoughts about God; they, and others like J. A. T. Robinson, by their affirmations of deity *in* Christ effectively deny the deity *of* Christ; their claims about his continuing influence effectively deny his bodily resurrection; and they state the forgiveness of sins in terms which deny his vicarious sin-bearing.[7] Nor, if these ideas were scotched, would the liberal snake be killed, for liberal theology is a parasite which lives by challenging received views in the name of reason, and its death in one form regularly heralds its rebirth in

---

[7] See, for justification of these statements, J. A. T. Robinson, *Honest to God*, London: SCM, 1963; *The Human Face of God* London: SCM, 1973; Don Cupitt in *The Myth of God Incarnate*, London: SCM, 1977, pp. 133 ff.; M. F. Wiles, *The Remaking of Christian Doctrine*, London: SCM, 1974; G. W. H. Lampe, *God as Spirit*, Oxford: Clarendon Press, 1977, and essay in A. Vidler, (ed.) *Soundings* Cambridge: CUP, 1962, pp. 173 ff.; Dennis Nineham in *The Myth of God Incarnate*, pp. 186 ff.

another.

There is thus little prospect of any church which allows liberal theological method ever being free of what to evangelicals appears major heresy; and it is clear that the Church of England today, in common with world-wide Anglicanism, understands its commitment to reason as the third strand of its principle of authority, along with Scripture and tradition, as legitimizing liberal method. Hooker, who gave Anglicans this formula, would certainly protest that this way of understanding it destroys his meaning completely, but nothing can be done about that now; we have gone too far. So the comfortable old concept of churchmen who are one on basics agreeing to disagree on secondary matters appears today to be a pipe-dream no longer bearing any relation to what is actually the case. The reality of Anglican comprehensiveness is quite different. It has become a matter of accepting theological bedfellows who may well have no more in common with you or with each other than the topics they discuss and the vocabulary they use for discussing them.

1.3. *Withdrawal?*

Seeing this, some have urged evangelicals in 'doctrinally mixed' churches to withdraw into a tighter fellowship where the pre-critical, pre-liberal view of Scripture is rigorously upheld and sceptical revisionism in theology is debarred. It has been said that failure to do this is as unprincipled as it is foolish. It is unprincipled, so the argument runs, because by staying in churches which tolerate heretics you become constructively guilty of their heresies, by your association with them; and it is foolish because you have not the least hope of cleaning up the theological Augean stables while liberals remain there. Withdrawal is the conscientious man's only option.

That the liberal theological method has come to stay in the Church of England is, as we saw, not open to doubt. That, for the present at least, it is the majority method among Anglican theologians is also clear. Though there is no reason to think that most Anglicans are liberals, the exposure given by the media to the provocatively unorthodox could easily give the impression that these men are on the intellectual growing edge of tomorrow's Anglican faith. Nor can this state of affairs be expected to change much in the foreseeable future; liberalism, which lives and can only live as a reaction against orthodoxy, will remain a cuckoo in the Anglican nest, and in each generation much theological energy will have to be invested in criticizing liberal criticisms of historic Christian belief. Accepting this is part of what is involved in being an Anglican evangelical today. All these, so far as man can foresee, are fixed points.

So, even if the separatist arguments are not thought cogent, the question presses: is the game worth the candle? Evangelical identity is trans-denominational, and Anglican evangelicals could find spiritual homes elsewhere if they had to: might they not be wise to do so, and wash their hands of the constant battle with the liberals, and invest their God-given mental energy elsewhere?

Half-way up the four flights of stairs leading to one of London's evangelical institutions there used to hang a card which said: 'Pause and Pray.' That is good advice too for folk faced with this specious summons to down tools and run. The genuine distress and frustration which evangelicals feel about the interminable theological incoherence of the Church of England gives the summons immediate appeal. But proverbial common sense tells us that though the grass the other side of the wall is always greener, we should look before we leap, lest we cut off our nose to spite our face and jump out of the frying-pan into the fire. Just as one cannot steer straight forward while looking back at what one is leaving, so one cannot trust reaction to induce right-mindedness. Even if not blind (as it often is), reaction is rarely far-sighted, and may lead to something worse than that from which it flees. 'Anywhere, provided it be forward' has been described as a philosophy for Gadarene swine, and 'anyhow, provided it be different' would be an axiom of anarchy. To see what to do about what one is against (in this case, a vicious doctrinal pluralism), one needs first to be clear what one is for. So our initial question must be: what sort of Church of England do evangelicals look for? Where do they think it should go, starting from where it is? What hopes and purposes have they for it? What policies do these purposes dictate? Here are the themes on which reflection should centre while separatist sirens sing their seductive song of flight from present troubles.

It will help us to think through these questions if for a moment we glance back at the Anglicanism of two evangelical patriarchs of yesterday, whom many in the Church of England have taken as role-models, and still do: Charles Simeon and J. C. Ryle. Granted, the methodological comprehensiveness of the Church of England today is, as we have begun to see, a relatively new thing, which the official apologia for comprehensiveness neither envisages nor covers, and neither of these men had to face it. Yet both belonged to a Church of England in which their evangelicalism was very far from being dominant or popular, and in that, at least, they were in the same boat as we are. What did they hope and work for in the disorderly Church of England of their day, and what was their attitude towards those doctrinal shortcomings which they detected? Let us see.

1.4. *Simeon and Ryle*[8]

First, their **profiles**. Simeon (1759-1836), son of a wealthy lawyer, brother of a baronet who sat in Parliament and of one of the Bank of England's directors, was an Eton boy who came to faith in Christ as an undergraduate at Kings College, Cambridge. Having graduated without examination and become a Fellow automatically, as Kingsmen did in those days, Simeon was ordained deacon at the age of 22. Three months later he asked his father to put his name forward to the Bishop of Ely for the vacant living of Holy Trinity, Cambridge, and amazingly he got it. There he stayed till his death

---

[8] On Simeon, see *Memoirs*, ed. W. Carus, 3rd ed., London, 1848; H. C. G. Moule, *Charles Simeon*, London, 1892; repr. IVP, 1948; Charles Smyth, *Simeon and Church Order*, Cambridge: CUP, 1940; Hugh Evan Hopkins, *Charles Simeon of Cambridge*, London: Hodder & Stoughton, 1977. On Ryle, see M. L. Loane, *John Charles Ryle*, London: James Clarke, 1953; J. C. Ryle, *A Self Portrait*, ed. P. Toon, Swengel, Pa.: Reiner, 1975; P. Toon and M. Smout, *John Charles Ryle: Evangelical Bishop*, Swengel, Pa.: Reiner, 1976.

54 years later, developing a ministry as preacher, student chaplain, nurturer of ordinands, pastor and educator of clergy, missionary organiser (Church Missionary Society, British and Foreign Bible Society, Society for Promoting Christianity among the Jews), resource person in clerical appointments, and finally purchaser of patronage, which led Macaulay to write: 'his real sway in the church was far greater than that of any primate.'[9] It was his happiness to see, in the last 25 years of his life, many signs that his kind of evangelicalism was establishing itself in the English middle and upper classes, largely through men whom he trained and advised.

John Charles Ryle (1816-1900) was also an Eton boy. Converted at Oxford, where he also gained a First Class degree, he was ordained when his father, a Cheshire banker, went bankrupt. For 39 years he served as a country parson, becoming an acknowledged evangelical leader through his tracts, books and power of speech; then at 64, 'set in his ways and his thoughts, past his best,'[10] he was made first bishop of Liverpool, where for two decades he worked manfully setting up a diocese that lacked money, buildings and human resources all along. Whereas Simeon's main ministry had been personal (for his 21-volume *Horae Homileticae*, 2,536 sermon outlines from Genesis to Revelation, was not equally influential), Ryle's chief influence was exerted through his pungent tracts and books, some of which are still in print today.[11]

The two Etonians make a fascinating contrast. Both were instinctive aristocrats, dignified and reserved to a degree, yet shrewd, energetic, articulate natural leaders, men of great personal force and pastoral wisdom, with views of Christianity and ministry

---

[9] Hopkins, *op. cit.,* p. 118. Simeon wrote: 'many of those who hear me are legions in themselves because they are going forth to preach, or else to fill stations of influence in society. In that view, I look on my position here as the highest and most important in the kingdom, nor would I exchange it for any other'; *op. cit.,* p. 86.

[10] Toon and Smout, *op. cit.,* p. 71.

[11] For example, Expository Thoughts on the four gospels; Christian Leaders of the 18th Century; The Upper Room; Holiness; Practical Religion; Old Paths; etc.

that were virtually identical. Here, however, the resemblance ends. Simeon, the Old Apostle as they called him, a warm-hearted though somewhat fussy and choleric bachelor, was always the eighteenth-century gentleman, with the elegant geniality that wealth and an assured position in society easily confer. Ryle, the Protestant Bishop, a man of granite with the heart of a child as his successor described him, was a raw-boned, big-voiced, blunt-spoken Victorian, brisk and brusque, tough-minded to the point of truculence, whose natural combativeness shone out in all he said and did – in short, a natural outsider. Not very sociable by nature, and scarred by the trauma of the family bankruptcy and 20 years of near-poverty that followed, plus the pain of losing two wives (the second of whom was an invalid for ten years) before he was 45, most folk found him abrupt and aloof, easier to admire from a distance than to relax with at close quarters. Ryle had better brains, more learning, and power on paper which Simeon quite lacked; Simeon had poise, charm and a genius for friendship which Ryle quite lacked, though there are places where Ryle's devotional writing communicates a depth of compassion which, from the evidence available, Simeon could not match. Simeon was evidently a sunny person, Ryle rather more severe. But both were great men, and when Anglican evangelicals divide, as they do, over which they prefer they tell us more about themselves than about either of them.

Second, their *principles*. Here they were together all the way. Both were English churchmen who understood Christianity in terms of the official Anglican formularies of the sixteenth and seventeenth centuries. Both saw real Christianity as based on the justification of sinners through grace by faith in the living Christ and his atoning death. Both applauded the Articles and Prayer Book for the model of doctrine and devotion which they provide. Both were moderate Calvinists, affirming election without speaking of reprobation and declaring universal as distinct from particular redemption. Both thought it good and right that the English national church should be established (Ryle wrote against disestablishment), and both regretted Dissent, though Ryle insisted that the Church was to blame for causing it. But as both understood preaching in terms of letting Scripture speak, and took its main message to be truths about the present relation of the living Triune God to sinners, and rang endless changes on these truths in their own preaching, so both were glad of Dissenters who preached the same message. The main concern of both was that Christ should be preached, never mind by whom.

Both saw the inherited Anglican system of endowed livings and paternalist patronage as providentially apt for furthering the gospel in England, especially in poor and ignorant communities, and as being fully justifiable on that basis; and both saw the main hindrance to the spread of the gospel in England as lying in failure to work the parochial system well enough. Simeon was up against non-residence and plurality, and clergy who were not 'serious' (an evangelical code-word in those days) about Prayer Book religion, who ridiculed those who were as 'enthusiasts' (i.e., fanatics), and who set forth ethics as the way to heaven. Ryle believed that Ritualistic crypto-Romanism, boiling down to trust in sacraments for salvation, and woolly Broad Church guesswork, boiling down to trust in sincerity for salvation, were establishing themselves as the preferred options of an increasing number of clergy, and ousting the gospel of the formularies. Both men, however, interpreted their situation in terms, not of apostasy, but of lack. They had confidence in the power of the gospel, once let loose, to make its way against these basically jejune alternatives and drive them back, and they saw it as their task to let the gospel loose every way they could.

Both were hopeful as they faced the future. This is less plain in Ryle, who unlike Simeon did not see his cause clearly triumph, and unlike Simeon again had in his mind a streak of pre-millennial pessimism, leading him to warn on occasion of wholesale apostasy before Christ's coming. Ryle voiced many forebodings of how the Church of England would collapse if doctrinal drift and disintegration went further, and urged constantly that evangelical faith could not be preserved without a fight. Yet he expressed hope too. The following extract gives the basic attitude which he maintained throughout.

You live in days when our time-honoured Church is in a very perilous, distressing, and critical position. Her rowers have brought her into troubled waters. Her very existence is endangered by Papists, Infidels, and Liberationists [disestablishmentarians] without. Her life-blood is drained away by the behaviour of traitors, false friends, and timid officers within. Nevertheless, so long as the Church of England sticks firmly to the Bible, the Articles and the principles of the Protestant Reformation, so long I advise you strongly to stick to the Church. When the Articles are thrown overboard and the old flag is hauled down, then, and not till then, it will be time for you and me to launch the boats and quit the wreck. At present, let us stick to the old ship.

Why should we leave her now, like cowards, because she is in difficulties and the truth cannot be maintained within her pale without trouble? How can we better ourselves? To whom can we go? Where shall we find better prayers? In what communion shall we find so much good being done, in spite of the existence of much evil? No doubt there is much to sadden us; but there is not a single visible Church on earth at this day doing better. There is not a single communion where there are no clouds, and all is serene ... But for all that, there is much to gladden us, more Evangelical preaching than there ever was before in the land, more work done both at home and abroad. If old William Romaine, of St. Anne's, Blackfriars, who stood alone with some half-dozen others in London last century, had lived to see what our eyes see, he would have sharply rebuked our faint-heartedness and unthankfulness. No! The battle of the Reformed Church of England is not yet lost, in spite of semi-popery and scepticism, whatever jealous onlookers without and melancholy grumblers within may please to say. As Napoleon said at four o'clock on the battlefield of Marengo, "there is yet time to win a victory." If the really loyal members of the Church will only stand by her boldly, and not look coolly at one another, and refuse to work the same fire engine, or man the same lifeboat – if they will not squabble and quarrel and "fall out by the way," the Church of England will live and not die, and be a blessing to our children's children. Then let us set our feet down firmly and stand fast .., man the pumps, and try to keep the good ship afloat. Let us work on, and fight on, and pray on, and stick to the Church of England."[12]

In other words, the Church of England was worth preserving; the misbelief of the day need not be fatal; if evangelicals would fight together for the gospel in the Church, they would succeed in keeping it there.

So to, third, the **programme** to which Simeon and Ryle committed themselves. Both constantly sought to do three things to reduce the doctrinal, devotional and practical defects of the Church of England as they found it:

(1)   To spread and defend the gospel by preaching, teaching and writing. (This was the hidden agenda of *Horae Homileticae*, as it was the explicit agenda of most of Ryle's written work.)

(2)   To establish clergy and ordinands in evangelical truth. (Simeon did this more obviously through student ministry and clergy conferences; Ryle did it indirectly, by backing evangelical theological colleges.)

(3)   To exert all possible influence to evangelical ends in the Church's wider life. (Simeon, living in an era when influence was chiefly a matter of whom one knew, cultivated dignitaries; Ryle urged against some of his peers that evangelicals should get stuck into the newly-born Church Congresses and Diocesan Conferences and the revived Convocations, and himself proposed reforming church courts, patronage and canon law, and transforming the Convocations into synodical government – all of which,

---

[12] *Holiness*, 1952 repr., London: James Clarke, pp. 307 f.; from a chapter entitled 'Wants of the Times'.

incidentally, has been done in the past generation, rather more than half a century after Ryle called for it.)

1.5.   *Past and Present*

How would Simeon and Ryle react could they see the Church of England today?

They would certainly be delighted that the number of clergy and congregations adhering to their kind of evangelicalism now seems greater than at any time in either of their lives. Simeon saw evangelical influence in the Church of England budding, Ryle thought, probably rightly, that overall he was watching it wither; neither saw evangelicalism blossom as it has blossomed in England during the second half of this century.

Both men would also be thankful to observe the strength of evangelical institutions and societies, the quantity and quality of evangelical printed matter, and the fact that evangelical theological colleges now train forty per cent at least of each generation of ordinands. Simeon would rejoice to see how widely his standards of parish ministry had established themselves; Ryle would be glad that the Church, instead of disintegrating as he feared it would through hostility from without coupled with centrifugal disunity and anarchy within, holds resolutely together, and the sense of unity and trust between churchmen of different schools who keep within the bounds set by the Creeds and Articles has notably grown in recent years.

Both men would wonder, perhaps, whether the quality of Anglican evangelicals today matches that of their predecessors one and two centuries ago. They might sense that we are little people with small souls. They might feel doubt as to whether, in their passion to worship God in the low-key twentieth-century way and in today's 'cool' English, evangelicals are holding firmly enough to the Bible-based Augustinianism of the Prayer Book and cultivating, along with their stress on fellowship with the Father, the Son and the saints, that due humility before God which bespeaks a sight of God's holiness and a true sense of sin. Present-day hymns and choruses in particular might make them scratch their heads at this point. In their own day, both were hot against respectable, easygoing, shallow people who played superficially with Christianity, and they would certainly wish to check up on us here.

Ryle, who constantly urged churchmen to study the Articles as the Church's confession of faith, would be amazed and, I expect, distressed that modern Anglican evangelicals attend to them so little. He would find it hard to believe that the 78-page *Nottingham Statement* (the findings of NEAC 1977) was a serious evangelical document, when it pronounced on the gospel, the Bible and Roman Catholicism, among other matters, without referring to the Articles once! But I think he would be glad to find that both the aggressions of Tridentine Roman Catholicism in England and popular patriotic reaction against it ('no popery!') – a scaremongering reaction with which Ryle himself largely identified, and at the time with reason – were things of the past. A realist in his own day, Ryle would appreciate that though the doctrinal gulf between Roman Catholicism and Protestant evangelicalism remains, the milieu in which to survey and debate it has changed dramatically since Vatican II, and for the better.[13] It is a poor tribute to Ryle's intelligence to suppose, as some seem to do, that he could not have allowed that a new situation has come to exist, nor understood it, nor welcomed and adjusted to it.

But what of Anglican comprehensiveness? Probably at first sight the range of beliefs and opinions tolerated among today's clergy, and the depth of indifference as to whether those who hold office as the Church's teachers believe one thing or another, would stagger both men. Simeon, who put on record his hope that *Horae Homileticae* would tend 'to weaken at least, if not eradicate, the disputes about Calvinism and Arminianism; and thus to recommend ... the unhampered liberality of the Church of England,'[14] died before the attempts of Tractarians and Liberals in Oxford to recover 'catholic' teaching and map out an up-to-date undogmatic intellectualism respectively had made any significant

---

[13] Cf. R. T. Beckwith, G. E. Duffield, J. I. Packer, *Across the Divide*, Basingstoke: Lyttelton Press, 1977.
[14] Carus, *op. cit.* p. 506. Simeon called himself a 'moderate Calvinist', p. 294.

impact. Apart from the Calvinistic issue, Simeon never had to engage directly with any theology different from his own save the natural man's heresy that we can be moral enough to be saved without faith in Christ; it is hard to envisage how he would have handled denials of the Trinity and Incarnation. Ryle had controverted the Romanizing distinctives of Ritualist theology and also the vague openness, optimistic, unspecific and clear only in being anti traditional, which came to mark Broad Church theorizing; he had argued against the idea that the Church of England had best become 'a kind of Noah's ark, within which every kind of opinion and creed shall dwell safe and undisturbed, and the only terms of communion shall be willingness to come inside and let your neighbour alone',[15] and had expounded his conviction that the wise bounds of Anglican comprehensiveness are those which are actually set by the Articles, Creeds and Prayer Book as understood in the sixteenth and seventeenth centuries. 'Let us be as broad as the Articles and Creeds, but not one inch broader,' he had written. 'If any one tries to persuade me that I ought to smile and look on complacently, with folded arms, while beneficed or licensed clergymen teach Deism, Socinianism or Romanism, I must tell him quite plainly that I cannot and will not do it ... I love my own Church too well to tolerate either scepticism on the one hand or Romanism on the other, and I think I am only doing my duty to my ordination vows in trying to "drive both away".'[16] Were he here today, to see Wiles' neo-Deism, Lampe's neo-Socinianism and the variety of faiths disclosed in the 1976 Doctrine Commission report Christian Believing, he would certainly judge the enlarged comprehensiveness which finds room for all this to be, in Sellar-and-Yeatmanese, a Bad Thing.

But what would they tell us to do about it? Ryle had seen heresy trials backfire (the acquittal in 1864 of Williams and Wilson, two contributors to Essays and Reviews, secured to English clergymen a legal right to treat parts of Scripture as unhistorical); he had learned from the Bell Cox prosecution in his own diocese

---

[15] Principles for Churchmen, London, 1884, p. xxiv.
[16] op. cit., p. 41.

(1886-7) how little you gain, and what goodwill you lose, by making martyrs of men who, however misled, are able, honest, hardworking and respected; he would be no more likely to recommend judicial proceedings than secession. What both he and Simeon could be expected to say, from what we know of them, is rather this:

(1)   We should remember that the defined faith, the historical heritage and the calling, evangelistic pastoral and prophetic, of the English national church remain what they were, despite the incursion of tolerated errors;

(2)   We should realise that the 'guilt by association' argument touches no one who explicitly dissociates himself from the errors concerned;

(3)   We should remind ourselves that by leaving the Church of England in disgust at its doctrinal disorders we should stand to lose more than we gained;

(4)   We should regard these errors, which are all well-meant efforts to restate the faith for today, in terms of deficiency – failure, that is, for whatever reason, to affirm the full gospel – and devote energy to filling in what they omit or refuse to say;

(5)   We should recognize that the best way to serve a church infected by error is to refute the error cogently in public discussion and debate, as Paul refuted the Galatian and Colossian errors, and Athanasius the Arian error, and Augustine the Pelagian error, and Luther Erasmus' semi-Pelagianism, and J. B. Lightfoot the errors of *Supernatural Religion*, and Eric Mascall the errors of Robinson's *Honest to God* and van Buren's *The Secular Meaning of the Gospel*.

(6)   We should resolve to pray for champions in scholarly debate who will be able to do this job effectively on the appropriate scale, and meantime say our own piece in public against the errors in question as clearly as we can; otherwise we shall find in ourselves an unquiet conscience,

and an ungodly desire to flee the Church of England, not because of the errors it tolerates, but only because of our own evading of the call to speak for God against them (as Jonah found himself wanting to flee from the presence of the Lord whose word he had refused to speak).

Whether or not I am right to put these words into the mouths of Simeon and Ryle, they are certainly the first things I want to say as we come now to grips with the over-tolerant comprehensiveness which appears as one of the leading vices of the present-day Church of England.

2. Anglican Comprehensiveness – A Likely Story?

One ingredient in today's Anglicanism – by which I mean the thought and practice of the Church of England with its worldwide daughters – is, as we saw, its claim to be comprehensive in a way that other traditions are not, and its confidence that this comprehensiveness is a fine thing. So far I have written as if it were just a matter of unlimited tolerance, sometimes of the intolerable, which would suggest that it is really less a glory than a shame. It certainly looks so from outside, and sometimes from inside too. Many Roman Catholics, Eastern Orthodox and non-Anglican evangelicals have thought it irresponsible and scandalous, and made no bones of saying so, and some of my own anger and misery at my church's complacent doctrinal disarray will have come through to my readers already. But there is, of course, at least in theory, more to comprehensiveness than this; though folk find it notoriously hard to get hold of just what.

Why is that? Because since the middle of the last century comprehensiveness has been paraded as an Anglican excellence from at least four distinct points of view, each observing it as a phenomenon and justifying it as a policy in a different way. When this fourfoldness is not discerned and consensus accounts of comprehensiveness are attempted, the results are so cloudy, unfocused and ambivalent that one can no more make sense of them than one can weave mist or sculpt custard. While it was to be expected that Anglican comprehensiveness would comprehend different ideas of itself, the effect, here as in other areas of plural Anglican thinking, is to induce a degree of theological glossolalia which Eeyore would have labelled a Confused Noise, and which is as maddening and bewildering to observers as it is embarrassing and frustrating to those whose own utterances are part of it. To make sense of this situation we have to separate out the four positions, locate them in the flow of Anglican history, show what distinct benefit each supposes itself to bring, and evaluate them on their separate merits. That is this chapter's task.

2.1. *Inclusiveness*

First, both historically and logically, comes the traditional understanding of comprehensiveness in terms of *calculated inclusion*. Here, comprehensiveness means a deliberate policy of so ordering the Church that it can be a spiritual home for all 'mere Christians' who do not insist on adding to the creed mediaeval and post-mediaeval novelties (papal claims, the Mass-sacrifice, etc.) or taking from it any of the biblical fundamentals which it contains.

Comprehensiveness in this sense was the aim of the Elizabethan settlement, which sought a church structure that might embrace the whole nation. The settlement took the form of a broad-based Protestant traditionalism circumscribed by the Articles and Prayer Book (two witnesses to a biblical fullness of faith and worship), the royal supremacy (the sign that the Church was national and established), and the historic episcopate (marking continuity in space and time with the church of earlier days). Being Reformational as against Papal and Anabaptist and on the eucharistic presence Reformed as against Roman Catholic and Lutheran (Article 28), the settlement could claim to embody the essence of New Testament and mainstream patristic Christianity; thus it displayed true catholicity of substance. The doctrine of the Articles was put forward as a sufficient minimum, leaving a great deal undefined, and no terms of lay communion were imposed other than *de facto* acceptance of the established order; thus a truly catholic inclusiveness was achieved as well.

Archbishop Parker, the first Elizabethan bishop, spoke of

the settlement in terms of 'golden mediocrity' (*aurea mediocritas:* 'a golden mean' is what we should say). With this may be bracketed the familiar idea of Anglicanism as a 'middle way' (*via media*). What these phrases point to is Anglican unwillingness to shape the Church in a way that either needlessly cuts loose from the past or needlessly cuts out Christians who would be part of it in the present. The *via media* was never, as is sometimes suggested, a tight-rope walk between Rome and the Reformation, nor between Romanism and Anabaptistry, but a pastorally-minded balancing of the claims of traditional faith and practice against the need to change for edification. Its spirit comes out in the opening sentence of the Preface to the 1662 Prayer Book: 'It hath been the wisdom of the Church of England, ever since the first compiling of her Publick Liturgy; to keep the mean between two extremes, of too much stiffness in refusing, and of too much easiness in admitting any variation from it.' The Cranmerian Prayer Book in its 1559 and 1662 revisions was in fact for centuries the chief instrument of comprehensiveness. Following time-honoured forms within a Reformed-Augustinian doctrinal frame, it was phrased with such breadth and resonance that it could delight a wide range of theological and liturgical palates. Long before the age of fish and chips the Book of Common Prayer was the Great British Invention, nurturing all sorts and conditions of Englishmen and holding the Church together with remarkable effectiveness.

The benefits sought through this policy of circumscribed inclusiveness were two: catholicity for the Church and unity, religious political and social, for the nation. Until the nineteenth century the policy seemed on the whole to be succeeding, despite the lapses of leadership which squeezed out the Puritans and Wesley's people in the seventeenth and eighteenth centuries respectively. But when Tractarians started to accuse the Church of defective catholicity because of what it jettisoned at the Reformation, and Newman to argue that for doctrine to remain the same it must constantly develop and change often, and liberals to deny that the Bible should be read as if God were its primary author, then not only Anglican unity but also the theological bases of the comprehensiveness policy itself were irrevocably undermined. For the policy rested on agreed acceptance of what the Bible, Creeds and Articles contain as normative revelation, or at least as catholic *theologoumena* that must not be spoken against. It expressed doctrinal modesty but not doctrinal indifferentism. Its demands and restrictions in matters of belief and behaviour were no less categorical for being minimal. But once substantial bodies of Anglican theological opinion began to question these demands on grounds of catholicity and truth, some wanting to augment and others to reduce what was common ground before, agreement that the Anglican set-up secured genuine catholicity became a thing of the past, and the Church changed overnight from a community unitedly proclaiming an achieved catholicity as the basis of its fellowship into one unitedly seeking such a basis but divided as to what, if anything, needed to be done to secure it. So for more than a century the Church has been a cockpit of debate between representatives of differently conceived catholicities trying to knock each other down and if possible out, or to elbow each other aside, or to find ways of taking into themselves the apparently opposed principles of the other views; and the debate continues.

In 1957 Alec Vidler wrote:

In these latter days the conception of Anglican comprehensiveness has been taken to mean that it is the glory of the Church of England to hold together in juxtaposition as many varieties of Christian faith and practice as are willing to agree to differ, so that the Church is regarded as a sort of league of religions. I have nothing to say for such an unprincipled syncretism ... the principle of comprehension is that a church ought to hold the fundamentals of the faith and at the same time allow for differences of opinion and of interpretation in secondary matters, especially rites and ceremonies. It is this principle that excluded .., those who believed too little, for instance any who did not accept the Creeds, as well as those who believed too much, for instance those who held that submission to the Bishop of Rome is necessary to salvation, or that Holy Scripture requires a Presbyterian form of church government and permits no other. Within these limits, which were secured by a uniform liturgy and by Articles of Religion which purported to be positive where Scripture was positive and reticent where it was not, it allowed for the maximum of flexibility and variety.[17]

Good words, and historically correct; but too many Anglicans have moved beyond this position for it to stand as an account of what Anglican comprehensiveness means today.

2.2.   *Integration*

Second comes F. D. Maurice's very influential reinterpretation of comprehensiveness as *integrative practice* – that is, the synthesizing in action of apparent theological opposites. Maurice (1805-72), an ex-Unitarian for whom the living Trinity was the key to everything, was both a speckled bird and a stormy petrel, a distinguished, original and isolated figure in the Church of England whose influence, gone as it seemed long before his death, has remarkably revived during the past half-century.[18] He lived when Anglican party strife was at its height, and his highly individual plea for a non-party understanding of the Church of England fell on deaf ears. Today it chimes in with what many wish to hear, so we should not perhaps be surprised when Maurice is hailed as a prophet for our time.

Maurice held that the God who bestows national characteristics appoints distinct destinies for various national churches, and that part of the Church of England's special calling is to synthesize in its ordered life of worship and ministry all the principles separately maintained as theoretical opposites by its three warring parties, evangelical, Tractarian and Broad Church. As he saw it, each party contends for a positive principle, to which it adds antithetical, negative, restrictive and sectarian notions in

[17] Vidler, *Essays in Liberality*, London: SCM, 1957, p. 166.
[18] On Maurice, see A. M. Ramsey, *F. D. Maurice and the Conflicts of Modern Theology*, Cambridge: CUP, 1951; Alec Vidler, *F. D. Maurice and Company*, London: SCM, 1966; W. Merlin Davies, *An Introduction to the Theology of F. D. Maurice*, London: SPCK, 1964; Torben Christensen, *The Divine Order*, Leiden: Brill, 1973.

order to form an exclusive system of thought (Maurice detested systems). Thus, evangelicals contend for salvation in Christ and muddy it with Calvinism, Tractarians contend for the God-givenness of the church and muddy their point with sacramentalist theory, and Broad Churchmen contend for freedom from bondage to intellectual systems of yesterday and link this with pleas to abolish the Articles and Prayer Book. But as Maurice saw it, all three positive principles were embodied already in the Church of England, with its creeds, sacraments, liturgy and ordained ministry, and the rest of each position could be safely dismissed as mistaken.

Maurice's contention at this point was that the union of the Triune God with mankind and the dominion of Christ over his church, together with the institutional means by which this union and dominion are furthered, are more basic to Christianity than any theological formulations. In one sense, of course they are, for things talked about are always basic to talk about them; but Maurice was meaning that the church is primarily institutional and only secondarily confessional, and that is much more disputable. His approving comment on the English Reformation, which Stephen Sykes quotes, shows his attitude: 'Here the idea of the Church as a Spiritual Polity ruled over by Christ, and consisting of all baptized persons, did, owing to various providential circumstances, supersede the notion of the Church, as a sect, maintaining certain options; or to speak more correctly, the dogmatical side of Christianity was here felt to be its accessory and subordinate side, and the ordinances, which were the manifestation of it as the law of our social and practical life, were considered its principal side. '[19]

Sykes judges that Maurice's view of Anglicanism has been 'theologically disastrous.' 'It must be said bluntly,' he explains, 'that it has served as an open invitation to intellectual laziness and self-deception ... the failure to be frank about the issues between the parties in the Church of England has led to an ultimately illusory self-projection as a church without any specific doctrinal or

---

[19] Maurice, *The Kingdom of Christ*, 1838, II. 338.

confessional position.'[20]   If ever we wondered whence came the facile idea, often met, that the Church of England is a liturgical rather than a confessional church, now we know.

It is hard to dissent from Sykes' verdict, and no less hard to accept Maurice's view of the Church of England. For

(1) in order to show how in Anglican practice the three party positions are complementary Maurice is forced high-handedly to redefine them in ways which neither evangelicals nor anglo-catholics can own.

(2) Maurice's view implies that the crusading Anglicanism of a Simeon-or Ryle-type evangelical, who wants to see the whole Church of England leavened with the gospel, is less authentically Anglican than that of a professedly anti-party institutionalist like himself.

(3) Since Maurice too was a theological crusader, advocating an account of universal redemption which neither evangelicals nor anglo-catholics could accept, and basing his institutionalism largely on it, he should really be seen as a one-man party, unlike others in having private theological reasons for not wanting to change the Church's constitution, but possessing no better claim to be a mainstream Anglican than anyone else.

(4) To suggest that in the English Reformation as a whole (as distinct from the reign of Henry VIII, which only saw its beginning) the issue of theological truth ('the dogmatical side of Christianity') was not primary is to part company with all exponents of what happened for the first hundred years after the event, not to mention most since. Granted, the Reformers sought a reformed catholicism, not a new start; granted too, no fully interlocked Anglican system like that of the Tridentine decrees or the seventeenth-century Westminster Confession was ever spelt out; nonetheless, what the Articles defined was set forth categorically and confessionally, to be the doctrinal standard for

---

[20] Stephen W. Sykes, *The Integrity of Anglicanism*, London: Mowbrays, 1978, p. 19.

interpreting Anglican liturgy, and it is idle to say it was not. 'We have all been taught' wrote Dr. Amand de Mendieta, 'that the English Prayer Book (1662) and the Thirty-nine Articles of Religion were deliberately so phrased that Catholics and Protestants alike could interpret them in their own way.'[21] Maybe we have, and maybe Maurice inspired much of the wishful thinking behind the statement; but of the Articles at any rate it is simply not true, and on this stubborn fact views of Anglicanism like Maurice's founder.

In sum: Maurice construed Anglican comprehensiveness as a genuine uniting of seeming opposites. He understood it as essentially a holding together, in a common frame of ministry and worship, of three types of folk who at the level of practical principle, that is, of faith and life as distinct from theology, were not basically disagreed, though they thought they were. Maurice believed he could see that their deepest contentions were complementary rather than contradictory. But this belief had in it less of prophetic insight than of theological oversight, for faith and theology cannot be thus separated. The Christ to whom each man's faith is a response is the Christ of the kerygma he believes, and to the extent that their understandings of the gospel vary different Christians serve different Christs, or at least differently conceived Christs. Had Maurice reflected on how the kerygmas of the three parties differed from each other, not to mention his own, he would surely have seen that his supposition of basic complementarity and harmony was superficial – though it has to be said that the decisiveness of differences of belief when held by users of the same liturgy is something which institutionalists both before and since Maurice have always found hard to appreciate. The final verdict on Maurice's vision of the Church of England must be that it was one of history's pleasanter pipe dreams. Would that it were so! But it was not so in Maurice's day, and it is not so now.

---

[21] E. Amand de Mendieta, 'From Anglican Symbiosis to Anglican Synthesis' in *The Anglican Synthesis*, ed. W. R. F. Browning, Derby: Peter Smith, 1964, p. 144.

2.3. *Tension*

Third in order comes the semi-official twentieth-century understanding of comprehensiveness as a state of *inner tension*, indeed frank disunity on some matters, which the Anglican Communion is providentially called to sustain because, first, out of it will some day emerge a richer wholeness (catholicity) than the Christian world yet knows and because, second, it qualifies the Anglican communion to act as a 'bridge church' bringing into unity with itself bodies which cannot at present find unity with each other. Inner incoherence is the price Anglicanism pays for the privilege of fulfilling its unique vocation in reintegrating Christ's divided church.

Sometimes this view is presented as an extension of Maurice's, and historically it may have developed in that way, but theologically it is a different thing altogether. Maurice looked back to Christ's founding of the church as his kingdom, and sought a way of harmony between warring Anglican groups by appeal to historically given institutions of the kingdom – sacraments, creeds, worship, ministry. This third view looks forward, anticipates new developments and states of things, and finds the meaning of present conflict in future prospects. Let me illustrate. Here, first, is Amand de Mendieta unveiling his vision for the church which he left the Roman communion to join.

> I am convinced that the historic mission or destiny of the Church of England, and, on a wider scale, the destiny of the world-wide Anglican Communion, is to make a theological and also a practical *synthesis* of Catholicism and Protestantism. Up to the present, we may say, the Church of England has too often been content with a more or less tolerant co-existence, a mere junta-position (*sic*) of different ideas, points of view, theologies, and practices, having no higher ambition than to keep a kind of precarious peace or rather truce, by letting sleeping dogs lie. But, to that extent, this so-called 'comprehensive' Church of England has failed to rise to the height of its historic and providential vocation. Our Church must bestir itself and *become* a

genuine dialectical Church ... a dialectical Church is committed to the view that all these views or particular theologies (Anglo-Catholic, Evangelical, Liberal) must *all* be transcended in a higher *synthesis*.[22]

And here is the Church Unity Committee of the 1948 Lambeth Conference reflecting on the tensions set up in reunion discussions with non-episcopal churches by the coexistence of different Anglican views of episcopacy.

> We recognise the inconveniences caused by these tensions, but we acknowledge them to be part of the will of God for us, since we believe it is only through a comprehensiveness which makes it possible to hold together in the Anglican Communion understandings of truth which are held in separation in other Churches, that the Anglican Communion is able to reach out in different directions and so fulfil its special vocation as one of God's instruments for the restoration of the visible unity of His whole Church. If at the present time one view were to prevail to the exclusion of all others, we should be delivered from our tensions, but only at the price of missing our opportunity and our vocation.[23]

It would be hazardous to speak either for or against this noble and hopeful vision, and I shall limit my comments to a review of some relevant facts.

First, it is a fact, and a happy one, that within the past thirty years the previously felt convictional and kerygmatic gap between the more conservative evangelicals and the more conservative anglo-catholics has shrunk.[24] On such matters as biblical authority,

---

[22] *op. cit.*, pp. 147, 153. The source of the 'dialectical church' idea is acknowledged to be H. A. Hodges in *Anglicanism and Orthodoxy: a study in Dialectical Churchmanship*, London: SCM, 1957.

[23] *The Lambeth Conference 1948*, London: SPCK, 1948, II. 50 f.

[24] For evidence of this, compare C. O. Buchanan, E. L. Mascall, J. I. Packer, Bishop of Willesden (G. D. Leonard), *Growing into Union*, London: SPCK, 1970, especially chs. 1-7, with *The Apostolic Ministry*, ed. K. E. Kirk, London: Hodders, 1946, which argued the necessity of episcopacy to the church's very

justification, the efficacy of baptism towards salvation, and the balance of preaching and eucharist in worship, there appears a convergence, which the charismatic, liturgical and evangelistic thrusts of our time continually help along. Today's evangelicals see that tradition has value as an aid to understanding Scripture and a safeguard against bondage to present-day cultural prejudice. Today's anglo-catholics see that tradition, which purports to embody and express biblical faith, must be judged by those very Scriptures which it interprets and applies. Most anglo-catholics allow that those who took evangelicals' *sola fide* to mean that justification is by feeling justified and that sanctification is unreal or unimportant, misheard. Most evangelicals perceive that the faith which catholics inculcate looks to the Christ whose salvation the sacraments display, and not to the sacraments without the Saviour. Evangelicals nowadays carry conviction when they profess concern for the universal visible church even though most of them still use the invisible-visible distinction to express their mind on the church's nature. Catholics nowadays have largely ceased to speak as if the church's existence depends on the prior and independent reality of the ordained ministry, even though they still go beyond evangelicals in their valuation of the historic episcopal succession. (The thought of the historic episcopate as a sign of the space-time continuity of Christ's ministry from heaven to his people has been found illuminating and unifying in some quarters.) Catholics have help evangelicals to see Christianity as the baptismal life; evangelicals have helped catholics to see it as a life of joyful assurance and expectant prayer. These are some of the more obvious points of convergence. How far the two bodies of opinion have really changed, and how far they are just hearing each other better, is a question on which views may vary, but that need not concern us. Somehow or other, convergence has come about, and for this we should he thankful.

But it is also a fact that in recent years an enormous gap has opened up between evangelicals and catholics on one side and,

being, and the report *Catholicity,* London: Dacre, 1947, which presented Protestantism as a total distortion of Christianity.

on the other, those liberals, heirs of the old Broad Churchmen, who since 1963, the year of *Honest to God*, have been called radicals – 'rads' against 'trads', or 'questers against 'resters'. The Bultmannite hermeneutic, which treats New Testament narrative and theology as so much culture-determined mythology, celebrating and evoking the ineffable impact of God upon us while telling us nothing of a divine-human redeemer at all, has bred a worldwide crop of Christian reconstructionists, all starting from a non-incarnational view of Jesus, all working with a unitarian idea of God seasoned with more or less of process-theology, all claiming that modern secular knowledge makes their type of view the only one possible, and all vigorously offsetting themselves from the categories and content of traditional belief. Many Anglicans, leading scholars among them, are in this camp. But the versions of Christian belief which the reconstructionists produce strike evangelicals and catholics as forms of unbelief, or at least of intellectual besetting sin,[25] and in relation to the fashion of thought that has produced them – which, please God, will pass, as fashions do – de Mendieta' s 'higher synthesis' is out of sight.

Finally, it must be said that events since 1948 have not given any obvious colour to the notion of Anglicanism's providentially appointed 'bridge' role. At home the Anglican-Methodist unity scheme has failed, partly because of its problematical Service of Reconciliation which maintained the rule, allegedly necessary to Anglican comprehensiveness, that non-episcopal clergy must receive the form of episcopal orders, and the subsequent multi-church discussions that produced the Ten Propositions do not seem to have been notably enlivened by Anglican magic. Overseas union schemes involving Anglicans have also collapsed or been put into store (New Zealand, USA, Canada, and several in Africa). In the world ecumenical movement Anglican leadership is a thing of the past. Pan-Anglican groups have talked to Lutheran, Roman Catholic and Orthodox representatives, and come under suspicion of saying different and

---

[25] This point is gently but firmly made by E. L. Mascall in *Theology and the Gospel of Christ*, London: SPCK, 1978.

incompatible things to different churches. If the confidence of the 1948 Lambeth Conference about the Anglican calling rested in any measure on the Anglican track record of significant ecumenical initiatives during the preceding half-century, the past thirty years must be said to have left the idea less credible than it was before. Whether the future will vindicate it remains to be seen; meantime, however, our right to invoke it in order to make current doctrinal cleavages easier to bear must be considered doubtful.

2.4. *Relativism*

The fourth and most recent way of understanding Anglican comprehensiveness is in terms of the belief, characteristic of the liberal tradition, that *theological relativism is inescapable*, and to make explicit provision for it is wise and healthy. No formulations of faith (it is urged) have finality; treat them as sacrosanct, and the church stagnates; but let reason, informed by contemporary culture, revise and reshape them, and the church will both appear relevant and be found enriched. Anglicanism, honouring reason in theology, has always instinctively made room for those who in the cause of truth and relevance have felt bound to challenge accepted formulations, and this comprehensiveness, whereby the Church in effect holds the ring for debate between advocates of the old and the new, is one main secret of Anglican resilience and vitality. So at least it is said.

To see what this viewpoint implies, we must be clear on some facts on which clarity is too often lacking.

First, the basis of all forms of this position is the hypothesis that no universally right way of thinking about God is given in Christianity. Evangelicals and anglo-catholics characteristically hold that there is a universally right way, given to us in the teaching and trains of thought found in the Bible. Catholics ordinarily make a point of adding that patristic tradition and conciliar definitions have authority as a guide to interpretation, setting limits within which all subsequent attempts to develop biblical thinking should stay. But for a century and a half those known as liberals, modernists and radicals have found this incredible. Unable to accept what might be called a Chalcedonian view of Scripture (i.e. that it is fully human as well as fully divine, and fully divine as well as fully human), they have doubted both the reality of the Chalcedonian Christ to whom the New Testament witnesses and the propriety of reading Scripture as more than a rag-bag of traditions, intuitions, fancies and mythology whereby good men celebrated and shared their sense of being in touch with God – a contact occasioned for New Testament writers by a uniquely godly man named Jesus. (This, of course, is how the sceptical conventions of biblical criticism, as practiced in the schools for over a century, would lead one to read Scripture were there not cogent reasons for taking higher ground.) That prophets and apostles no less than creeds and churches can all be wrong on questions of reality and truth, is plank one in the liberal platform. Scripture and the Christian literary heritage are certainly stimulating, inspiring and effective in communicating God, but that does not make them true. So the constant endeavour of the liberal fraternity from the start has been to go behind and beyond biblical witness to reformulate the faith in terms which to them, as modern men, seem truer, clearer and less inadequate (whether evolutionist, idealist, panentheist, deist, existentialist, Marxist; sociological, psychological, syncretistic; or whatever).

In this they break both with the Latitudinarians of the seventeenth and eighteenth centuries, who saw human orthodoxies as mere logic-chopping but the Bible as infallible truth, and with all who have upheld the idea of an agreed core of fundamentals. Sykes notes how Gore, the pioneer liberal catholic, met Anglican modernism with the demand that all articles of the creed be treated as fundamentals, including Jesus' virgin birth and resurrection, both of which (said Gore) historical enquiry confirms. 'But' comments Sykes 'the question he did not tackle satisfactorily was whether a Church could demand that all its clergy adopt the same conclusions on historical matters. In view of the very large quantity and weight of dissentient voices in Gore's own day and since, it would be a little absurd to claim that Gore's position on this matter was in any sense characteristically Anglican.'[26] Certainly, for today's liberals there are no fixed fundamentals; everything, not excluding the doctrine of God – indeed, some say, that first – is regarded as in principle open to review and change.

Second, the liberal presence guarantees genuine contradiction of views. Sykes rightly says that it is a presence rather than a party; liberals have no united platform or policy, for they hold in common only the negations noted in the last two paragraphs, plus the sifting, reshaping methodology which these negations entail. They agree only in what they are against; beyond this it is every man for himself. 'It is a very obvious fact that modern radicals in the Church of England neither form a cohesive group nor identify themselves with the earlier modernist movement.'[27] Sykes blames Maurice for leading Anglicans to think of liberals as a party in the Church parallel to the other two. He notes that 'a "liberal" theological proposal is always in the form of a challenge to an established authority, and thus necessarily implies a dispute about the appropriate norms or criteria for any theology whatsoever.' He notes too that 'it is impossible to be merely a "liberal" in theology; one's theology ... will be liberal in as much as it is a modification of an already existing type' – liberal catholic, liberal evangelical, or even liberal latitudinarian.[28] And he rightly stresses that any church in which liberals do their thing, querying the traditional and jettisoning the conventional, will have to endure real divergences of belief as some negate what others affirm and affirm what others cannot but negate. As he observes, 'Maurice's theory of comprehensiveness is utterly inadequate to account for this situation, and to persist in using it is a dangerous form of ecclesiastical self-deception.'[29]

Third, the liberal method has gained acceptance in Anglicanism, as in most other large Protestant churches. When in 1862 two of the authors of *Essays and Reviews* were tried for

[26] Sykes, *op. cit.,* p. 23.
[27] *op. cit.,* p. 31.
[28] *op. cit.,* pp. 32f.
[29] *op. cit.,* p. 33.

heresy, most of the novelties they affirmed were held not to be contrary to the doctrine of the Church of England. When in 1921 Gore urged that modernists be disciplined for sitting loose to the creed, the response of the Archbishop of Canterbury, Randall Davidson, was to set up a commission to report on the state of doctrine in the Church of England, and its report, by acknowledging the liberals' contribution to the thought-life of the Church, was, says Sykes, an 'unambiguous victory' for them.[30] The 1976 Doctrine Commission report, *Christian Believing*, distinguishes four attitudes of Anglicans to the creeds which they recite in worship. Some embrace them as norms, 'classical crystallizations of biblical faith'. Some recite them, despite reservations about their content, as a way of professing solidarity with the historic church. Some 'can neither affirm nor deny the creeds, because they look to the present rather than to the past to express their faith, and attach most importance to fresh understandings of that continuing Christian enterprise which has its origin in Jesus.' Some feel the fallibility of creeds and cannot in principle regard them as expressing their loyalty to Jesus and the Creator, so feel uninvolved with them. The first attitude is characteristic of evangelicals and catholics, the other three of liberals. Coexistence is painful, but 'the tension must be endured,' says the report; the church gains more from responsible debate between those who hold these points of view than it could gain by ruling any of them out.[31] Clearly liberalism has come to stay.

Fourth, all forms of liberalism are unstable. Being developed in each case by taking some secular fashion of thought as the fixed point (evolutionary optimism, historical scepticism, Marxist sociology, or whatever), and remodelling the Christian tradition to fit it, they are all doomed to die as soon as the fashion changes, according to Dean Inge's true saying that he who marries the spirit of the age today will be a widower tomorrow. It is not always realised that the history of the past century and a half is

---

[30] *op. cit.*, p. 30. The report was entitled *Doctrine in the Church of England*, The Report of the Commission on Christian Doctrine appointed by the Archbishops of Canterbury and York in 1922, London: SPCK, 1938.

[31] *Christian Believing*, London: SPCK, 1976, pp. 35-39.

littered with the wreckage of dead liberalisms. Though liberalism as an attitude of mind (going back at least to the Renaissance, if not indeed to the temptation of Eve) has persisted, and persists still, particular liberalisms have so far been relatively short-lived, and can be expected to continue so. Some liberals cheerfully acknowledge this and never treat their current opinions as more than provisional, anticipating that they may think differently next week. Others clearly cannot bear this prospect, and respond to factors which undermine their present opinions in the manner of King Canute forbidding the tide to come in; but the former group are more clear-headed. They measure the health of theology by its fertility in producing new options alternative to old ones, and value Anglican doctrinal tolerance (which they equate with comprehensiveness) because it removes all restraints on innovation.

Anglicans with a juster idea of what is given in Christianity see the matter rather differently. They judge of the health of theology by such criteria as fidelity to Scripture and in particular to the truths of incarnation and mediation, and they find the endless shifts of the liberal kaleidoscope reminding them irresistibly of the folk whom the New Testament describes as always learning and never able to come to a knowledge of the truth (2 Timothy 3:7). Only by an agnostic judgment of charity can they treat exponents of non-incarnational Christianity as Christians, and they see all such doctrine as weakening the church and threatening men's spiritual welfare. Though thankful that no particular liberalism can hope to last, their hearts still cry, 'Lord, how long?'

2.5. *Anglicans Assorted*

From the foregoing survey we can now see precisely what Anglican comprehensiveness amounts to in the year of grace 1981. We perceive that, though all agree that catholicity requires as wide a comprehensiveness as the Christian revelation will allow, there is no common mind on how the current breadth of doctrinal toleration should be regarded.

Some still define Anglicanism in terms of the

fundamentals set forth in the creeds and Articles, and challenge the propriety of clergy who sit loose to these ministering in the Church of England. Thus, for example, in 1977 the Church of England Evangelical Council declared:

> If, then, a time comes when a clergyman can no longer conscientiously teach something central to his church's doctrine (such as the personal deity of Jesus) which he has solemnly undertaken to teach, we urge that the only honourable course open to him is to resign any post he occupies as an accredited teacher of his church ... in the last resort (i) if a central Christian doctrine is at stake, (ii) if the clergyman concerned is not just questioning it but denying it, (iii) if he is not just passing through a temporary period of uncertainty but has reached a settled conviction, and (iv) if he refuses to resign, then we believe the bishop (or other leader) should seriously consider withdrawing his licence or permission to teach in the church.[32]

Others continue to believe (though, it seems, myopically) that all Anglicans are 'really' united, whatever their views, by virtue of their common loyalty to the Anglican communion as a going concern, and that a transcendent synthesis of what now appear as contradictory theologies either exists already or will exist some day. So they decline to be troubled by any outbursts of apparent heterodoxy, or to be moved by others' distress at them, judging that the heretics' continuing loyalty to the institution suffices to excuse any unfortunate things they say. There is no official attitude to public heterodoxy among Anglicans, but this is the common attitude of officials in the Church's administrative hierarchy.

Finally, a strident minority, whose noise-to-numbers ratio in the Church of England reminds one of the 3,000-strong British Humanist Association in Britain's domestic affairs, insists that any ascription to Jesus and his church of any kind of ultimate significance should be accepted as a legitimate Christian option,

---

[32] *Truth, Error and Discipline in the Church*; issued by the Church of England Evangelical Council, London: Vine Books, 1978, pp. 12f.

since the focusing of this significance is what Christian theology with its inescapable conceptual relativism is really all about.

Advocates of the three positions understand Scripture and practise theology in such different ways that genuine communication between them is next to impossible. They are to each other very different animals, and from this standpoint comparing the Church of England which contains them to Noah's ark is not facetious but apt.

I do not suppose I am the only one for whom Anglicanism still means identifying with official doctrinal standards (creeds and Articles, historically understood), and appreciating the Anglican heritage – the 1662 Prayer Book, beside which modern alternatives seem so feeble and wet; the ethos of a biblically reformed and informed traditionalism; the concern for catholicity which makes Anglicans eager to embrace everything of value in other churches' traditions, and the hatred of sectarianism which makes them hostile to narrow one-sidedness; the practical, pastoral orientation of theological enquiry; the long-suffering tolerance which waits for things to be thoroughly discussed, lest consciences be wounded or truth squandered; and so forth. Nor do I suppose I am the only one whose active Anglicanism expresses, not complacency at what the Church is today, but hope of what it may be tomorrow, when (please God) it reapprehends its heritage and is renewed in so doing. How should Anglicans of my sort, for whom so often it is only the Anglican ideal that makes actual Anglicanism bearable, view the present state of doctrine in the Church of England? The next chapter will try to answer that question.

3. Anglican Comprehensiveness – The Hard-Made Decision

'The hard-made decision' is Beethoven's phrase; he wrote it in capitals (DER SCHWER GEFASSTE ENTSCHLUSS) above the last movement of his last quartet (Op. 135, in F). With it he wrote a question-and-answer motto over the two three-note phrases which start its main theme: 'Must it be? It must be!' (*Muss es sein? Es muss sein!*) It was his last word on the topic about which for a quarter of a century he had been sending the world musical messages, the Eroica symphony being the first. That topic was the creative and even joyous acceptance of circumstances so far from ideal that you feel them threatening to crush you. Beethoven, the first great composer to see music as personal communication, spent his best years focusing in some thirty transcendent masterpieces aspects of that spirit which, when 'fate knocks at the door', refuses to be crushed, but regains strength and fights back to triumph – not over the pressure, but under it. It was fitting that eight months after finishing the quartet, and following two days of unconsciousness, Beethoven should be momentarily roused by an enormous thunderclap and die open-eyed, his clenched fist raised 'with a very serious, threatening expression'. The quartet, however, is peaceful. The motto, says Sullivan, 'is a summary of the great Beethoven problem of destiny and submission. But Beethoven ... treats the old question here with the lightness, even the humour, of one to whom the issue is settled and familiar ... the portentous question meets with a jovial, almost exultant answer, and the ending is one of perfect confidence.'[33] Living daily with acute frustrations – deafness, his ears 'whistling and buzzing constantly'; loneliness; unsteady health; poverty; the dirty, depressing muddle of his bachelor home; and a failed relationship with his nephew, the one person on whom he lavished love and from whom he sought love in return – Beethoven was voicing contentment, not indeed with pain and grief as such, but with the creativity which his pain and grief had enhanced. 'Must it be? It must be!' As if to say: I would not have shaped my task as circumstances have now shaped it, but I accept it, and find life to be satisfying and worthwhile as I rise to it. On which the proper comment is the dictum of Ecclesiastes: 'There is nothing better for a man than that he should eat and drink, and find enjoyment In his toil' (2:24, cf. 3:22). How true that is.

In this chapter I shall suggest that fruitfulness for oneself and others may come from a comparable 'hard-made decision' to

---

[33] J. W. N. Sullivan, *Beethoven*, Harmondsworth: Penguin, 1949, p. 155.

commit oneself to Anglicanism despite its doctrinal disorders. I shall not, however, suggest that this is in any way a heroic gesture. The Beethoven of Op. 135 would have laughed at the idea that his acceptance of the inevitable was heroic; maybe he thought so in his Eroica days,[34] but at the age of 56 he took himself less seriously. This was how it had to be, and that was that. Mature Christians who toil and endure for God do not think themselves heroes either; for them too it is all in the day's work, as God helps them to do what has to be done next. It was so with Paul. Once, for pastoral reasons, he felt obliged, against his preference, to catalogue the hair-shirt conditions of his life as if he was boasting about them. ' ... Far more imprisonments, with countless beatings ... once I was stoned. Three times I have been shipwrecked ... in danger from rivers, danger from robbers, danger from my own people, danger from the Gentiles ... danger from false brethren ... And, apart from other things, there is the daily pressure upon me of my anxiety for all the churches ... Who is made to fall, and I am not indignant?' (2 Cor. 11:23-29). But he felt awkward saying all this, lest he seem to be parading himself as a hero; as he soon found opportunity to repeat (for he had said it at length already in the earlier part of the letter), he was no more than a man who in conscious weakness knew the strengthening power of his Lord (12:5-10; cf. 11:30, chaps. 1-5~). And all who, with Paul, labour up to the limit for Christian conversion and nurture, and against unbelief, misbelief and sin in the church, know themselves to be in the same boat. They do what they have to do, in the strength of the Lord who moved them to attempt it, and give him the glory for whatever goes right.

3.1. *Anglican by Choice*

First let it be stressed, now as I start my argument, that Anglicans today are so by choice. This is because the visible church is now split into overlapping denominations; you opt for the one you prefer. There was no such choice in apostolic or patristic days, for then each local congregation was seen as an outcrop and

---

[34] Cf. Sullivan, *op. cit.*, pp. 60-77, where the Heiligenstadt Testament of 1802 is printed in full.

microcosm of the one world church, and being one with your own local group was part of the definition of being a Christian. Nor was there any such choice in the Middle Ages, when one communion (based on either Rome or Constantinople) existed in each Christian country and all were routinely brought into it by infant baptism. After the Reformation a choice of sorts existed, but English patriotism was held to prescribe allegiance to the national church, and for centuries Dissent, whether of Roman recusants or Protestant nonconformists, was regarded as, if not actually treasonable, at least somewhat subversive and schismatic. But since the Lambeth Conference of 1920 issued its 'Appeal to all Christian People', Anglicans everywhere have learned to respect non-Anglican churches for the Christianity they maintain, and this creates an open-choice situation with regard to Anglicanism itself.

In North America, where no church is established or given national-church status and the Anglican church is not the largest, newspaper adverts invite you to attend 'the church of your choice'. In England the Church of England remains the established national church, seeking to pastor the nation in Christ's name, and is far the largest Christian body, yet those Englishmen who attend church at all do in fact go to 'the church of their choice' as truly as North Americans do. Anglicanism as the English folk-religion, a patriotic observance or a social formality, is almost dead. Today's Anglicans choose to be Anglicans rather than anything else for Christian rather than social or secular reasons – that is, they become and stay Anglicans because they find in Anglicanism a satisfying expression of Christianity. Church allegiance has thus become really if regrettably (and not all regret it), a matter of Christian liberty – with which goes Christian responsibility, the duty of making the best possible decision, and from which, on the principles of Romans 14, comes Christian diversity as folk decide differently. It would be shallow to object here that church allegiance is usually determined by inertia, the habit of staying put, for in a matter of this kind inertia is itself a choice. People opt for the church which seems actually or potentially to have what they look for in terms of doctrinal commitment, worship style, preaching and teaching, pastoral care, group activities, opportunities of service, episcopacy (this still counts heavily for some), nearness to home, or whatever. The layman's choice will naturally be determined by the qualities of the particular congregation he joins, and rightly so; he is, after all, choosing his spiritual home. Yet he has some responsibility to evaluate the denomination to which it belongs, just as local government electors should weigh the party platform of candidates whom they know and trust as persons before giving them their votes. In both cases, personal affinity may rightly end up as the deciding factor, but the other should at least be thought about. Clergy, however, being willy-nilly denominational officers, have to weigh the denominational issue more carefully.

I maintain that a man with his eyes open to the full range of Anglican doctrinal pluralism may yet responsibly choose to be an Anglican, even an Anglican minister, though it may be a hard-made decision bringing misery as well as fulfilment. I do not maintain (I had better say this outright) that choosing to be an Anglican is a virtue, or that choosing not to be one or not to stay one is a vice. Choice, we saw, is necessary, and anyone may conclude that, rather than be Anglican, Methodist, Baptist Union or United Reformed (all which bodies are doctrinally mixed), he should join one of the smaller groups (Brethren, Pentecostals, Fellowship of Independent Evangelical Churches, Reformed Baptists, Free Church of Scotland, etc.) which debar from the ranks of their teachers anyone holding 'critical' views of Scripture or rejecting major evangelical tenets. To be sure, some think these smaller bodies purchase doctrinal purity at the price of theological stagnation, and are cultural backwaters out of touch with society around, just as some think Anglican allegiance is an unholy identification with cultural privilege, ecclesiastical worldliness and theological indifferentism. But these matters are arguable both ways, and neither estimate need be accepted. More important is respect for the other man's deliberate decision, whether or not it coincides with your own.

He who chooses Anglicanism finds himself, as we have seen, in a large, loose, complex church structure with a conservative tone but a seemingly endless willingness to tolerate cultured heretics. It has an official doctrinal commitment to the sufficiency of 'God's Word written' (Articles VI, XX), and a liturgical custom of reading Scripture in large quantities, larger perhaps than any other mainline church can match. But it is currently split on what the Bible means, so that the range of beliefs found among its teachers is startlingly, not to say scandalously, wide, and recognizable evangelical faith, whether protestant, anglo-catholic or charismatic in colouring, is a minority phenomenon. Yet God's church, of which the Church of England is professedly part, is charged to guard the deposit of apostolic teaching, to adhere unwaveringly to the New Testament gospel (cf. Galatians 1:6-9; 2 Timothy 1:12 f., 2:2), and so to prove itself 'the pillar and bulwark of the truth' (1 Timothy 3:15). How then do evangelicals who, whether for reasons already given or for others, choose Anglicanism view the doctrinal free-for-all which Anglican comprehensiveness has become? Often they bemoan it, as I have been doing myself; what, then, makes it possible for them to accept it? Have they ceased to regard faithful stewardship of God's revealed truth as the church's calling, and their own too? Or are they compromising their principles by ducking the issue? Or what? How can they have a good conscience, living cheek-by-jowl with so much heterodox teaching? These are proper and pressing questions; no Anglican evangelical can be excused from facing them, nor commended if he tries or manages to get along without an answer to them.

Here in a nutshell is my answer, for what it is worth. I submit that evangelicals were right to approve the older type of comprehensiveness, based on common acceptance of the fundamentals of the creed, but that they cannot and, for a fact, do not commend or condone what that historic comprehensiveness has now turned into. They accept it reluctantly and with sorrow, as in a fallen world and an imperfectly sanctified church they accept much else reluctantly and with sorrow. They accept it not as one of

Anglicanism's special goodies but as the unavoidable result of one of Anglicanism's other qualities, namely its desire to rule out no questions and clamp down on no discussions, but to give every viewpoint which claims, however freakishly, to be in line with Scripture and reason, opportunity to make its claim good, if it can. Approving this quality as a mark of both human and Christian maturity, they are prepared to show conscientious goodwill to a good deal of experimental theology which would, perhaps, be looked at askance in doctrinally unmixed churches.   But in accepting Anglicanism's present doctrinal plurality in this way their conscience is good and their commitment to doctrinal purity as an ideal remains uncompromised, for:

(1) They see that in the providence of God much insight, stimulus and help in understanding spins off from work done by good scholars whose claim to be interpreting Christianity is marred by some seemingly heterodox opinions. From this they conclude that the church gains more from continuing to accept these men on the basis of their own good intentions, while looking to its orthodox scholars to correct any oddities, than it could do by officially outlawing them and declining to pay serious attention to their work. The formalist idea of orthodoxy as a matter merely of keeping yesterday's dogmatic formulae intact seems inadequate to evangelicals, vigorously as they often defend these formulae; the orthodoxy that evangelicals seek is one which, while wholly faithful to the substance of the biblical message, will be fully contemporary in orientation and expression, and they know that to this end experiments in re-statement must be allowed. They know too that in matters exegetical and theological the profoundest perception does not always belong to those who aim to be 'sound' and 'safe', and they are sensitive to the narrowing effect which restricting oneself to what is 'sound' and 'safe' can have on the mind. So, because of the great potential benefit of what the theological explorers do, Anglican evangelicals think it right to be patient with them, despite what appear to be dropped bricks; you do not shoot explorers, any more than pianists, when they are doing their best. Evangelicals perceive that much of the exploring is done on the basis of the academic freedom which all scholars outside

Communist countries claim – that is, freedom to follow the argument wherever it seems to lead and to publish novel notions, hypothetically held, to see how the scholarly world reacts to them. Also, evangelicals perceive that if in the course of these explorations real fundamental heresy is put out, wittingly or unwittingly, more benefit comes to the church from public analysis and refutation (as when Paul trounced the Galatian and Colossian heresies, and Augustine the Pelagian heresy, and John Owen the Socinian heresy) than from any use of the big stick on the offending author. The words quoted above from the C. E. E. C. document showed that they do not rule out discreet use of the big stick as a last resort on heretical clergy guilty of what used to be called contumacy (and for this there is biblical precedent: see 1 Timothy 1:20; 2 John 9-11). But evangelicals think that, as the same document goes on to say: 'The most effective way to restrain and correct error Is not by a resort to repressive measures but by a convincing commendation of the truth, with a corollary exposure of error in all its arbitrariness and incoherence.'[35]

In a mature Christian community such as the Church of England seeks to be, one which declines any Idea of infallible Popes, bishops or preachers but gives the Bible to the laity so that the whole community together may judge on matters of faith, demonstration through debate naturally and necessarily becomes the basic form of discipline in Christian doctrine. The risks of the procedure (unending pluralism, constant muddle, public vacillation and embarrassment) are high; however, its benefits (ripe convictions emerging from a long hard look at alternatives) make the risks worth taking.

(2) Evangelicals see it as part of their own task in the Church of England to serve present and future Anglicans (not to say members of the doctrinally-unmixed bodies mentioned earlier) by themselves tackling off-key views in debate and showing them inadequate. While welcoming what insights they find in the work of the heterodox, they approach the excrescences of current

---

[35] *Truth, Error and Discipline in the Church*, p. 14. The earlier quotation is on p. 160 above.

Anglican over-comprehensiveness from the standpoint of the original comprehensiveness to which they adhere as their ideal, and what seems to cut at fundamentals they attack. They do not passively accept all the disorder they find. Nor do they accept that they are guilty by association of the errors they oppose (a nonsense notion, which has been given an unhappy airing during the past two decades); nor do they accept that they are settling for a situation in which no doctrinal discipline operates. They urge, rather, that discipline (which means training – Latin, *disciplina*) is in Scripture a primarily pastoral concept, and that the kind of pastorally-oriented controversy in which they engage is the basic form of discipline in the doctrinal realm.

Ecumenical idealists on the one hand and evangelical separatists on the other think it scandalous that the visible church should be racked with conflicts about belief, and labour for a state of affairs in which their neck of the woods, at any rate, shall be free from it. Conflict over doctrine, however, and fundamental doctrine at that (the person, work, place and sufficiency of Jesus Christ our Saviour), kept occurring in the apostolic church, as witness the New Testament letters, and we find Paul writing to the Corinthians: 'No doubt there have to be differences among you to show which of you have God's approval' (1 Corinthians 11:19, NIV). Implicit in his words seems to be the far-reaching principle that God will regularly allow divisions of one sort or another to enter the churches, as they had entered the Corinthian community, so that the different consequences for spiritual enrichment or leanness of different beliefs and ways of behaving may become plain. Certainly, evangelicals in the Church of England do not suppose that their conflict with well-meant misbelief will be over until the Lord comes. But they are not discouraged. They see this task as part of the package deal which they accepted when they chose Anglicanism, and they know that for them this choice was the 'best buy'. A hard-made decision? Maybe; but not one to regret, for all the burdens it brings.

It is important not to miss the force of this reasoning by falling victim to the sectarian idea, sometimes met, that evangelicalism, being Christianity at its purest, ought to practice self-sufficiency in theology, taking nothing from the mixed bag of Roman Catholic, Orthodox, Anglo-Catholic and liberal Protestant thought on the grounds that nothing in that bag can help evangelicals in the least. Were this idea sound, the case for patience with the intermittently heterodox would be less strong; but the idea is not sound. I for one regard the evangelicalism outlined in the opening paragraphs of this essay as the purest Christianity that the world has seen since apostolic times, and in that sense I affirm Christianity to be evangelicalism and vice versa. But it does not follow that adherents of other mutations of Christianity, mutations which seem less close overall to the spirit, belief and thrust of the New Testament, have nothing to teach me on this or that particular point – nothing, that is, which I could not have learned from some evangelical source. Nor does it follow that I serve God best by assuming there are no new truths, or new applications of truth, that wait to break forth from his holy Word, so that as a teacher in the church I need only repeat traditional evangelical positions and I shall have done my job. The truth is rather this: Theology is an ongoing corporate enterprise which in principle involves the whole church. It is an enterprise through which everyone's understanding of what God has revealed is again and again enlarged. It proceeds by dialogue with past and present attempts to spell out that revelation, dialogue through which Scripture actually evaluates the various attempts made to expound it. We all need to examine and re-examine by Scripture whether our own traditions, as well as those of others, are true and adequate (two questions, not just one); and the late B. B. Warfield, as doughty a Reformed traditionalist as the world has seen, was right when he said in conversation that the theologian must be like the busy bee, always moving around gathering raw material for honey from all sorts of flowers. So it is best, in these days when identifying the main stream of Christian belief is not a problem (it was different in New Testament times), not to treat those who seem heretical on one key point in a way that keeps the church from benefiting by their insight on other points. Hence the preferable course is exposition and debate.

3.3. *A Sense of Proportion*

I have tried in this essay to formulate an overall approach to the over-comprehensiveness which for many is the saddest aspect of the present day Church of England. Not all the many, incidentally, are evangelicals; there can be few Anglican catholics who do not feel equal misery at the freedom to sit loose to fundamentals which some theologians claim in the name of contemporary reinterpretation of the faith. But we must not get this out of proportion. The handful of distinguished radicals who are at present catching the public eye are as nothing compared to the solid body of Anglicans, lay and clerical, for whom Scripture remains God's message to us, who identify the Christ of faith with the Jesus of history and the Jesus of history with the Jesus of the gospels, and who still value the creeds as declaring the key facts on which faith rests. Far more exposition of the evangelical faith by Anglicans goes into print than of radical alternatives, and far more renewal of spiritual life is experienced where Christ is proclaimed from the Bible in the old way than where radical notions have come. (Radicals talk much of renewal, but the pastoral barrenness of their doctrine is a byword). By God's mercy the Church of England, though disorderly, is far from dead, and there is no solid reason to suppose that those Anglicans who contend for the historic gospel are fighting a losing battle.

We looked earlier at J. C. Ryle, the evangelical champion whose episcopate began in 1880, just over a century ago. Folk sometimes guess what he might say could he inspect the Church of England now, and I shall add my guess to theirs. Indeed, I made my guess several pages back. He would note how the Church has shrunk and lost influence; he would tell us that it looks more like a doctrinal Noah's ark than ever. But he would also thankfully record that his often expressed fear that the Church would split and sink had proved unfounded; that there was in fact more unity on essentials than in his day, and more concern for evangelism, and more respect for each other among the parties, that there was less Romanizing and less quarrelsomeness than he knew, and more esprit de corps. Our radicalism might well make him blink, but he would see it, despite the self-confidence of its exponents, as what it is – an aggregate of unstable minority positions, for none of which can long life be expected. Despite its presence he would, I think, take heart, and tell all evangelicals to do the same.

But the argument I have been using to justify the hard-made decision of Anglican allegiance is one of principle – namely, that the way in which Anglican tolerance obliges you to cope with Anglican doctrinal disorder is, though taxing, the best way both for you and for the Church as a whole; and this argument does not draw any of its force from rosy hopes for the future. On the doctrinal front I do not in fact entertain rosy hopes. Reduced Christianities, like the poor, will no doubt always be with us, and it is not my thought that a good heave now would rid us of them for all time. I simply urge that the way of dealing with them which has been described will continue to be the right and proper way, however angry or upset their existence makes you feel, and whether the Church seems for the moment to be gaining doctrinal purity or losing it. The motto of Oak Hill Theological College, where I was once privileged to teach, is 'Be Right and Persist', and that is the practical summons to which, as it seems to me, my argument of principle leads.

LATIMER PUBLICATIONS

LATIMER PUBLICATIONS

Latimer Publications

CPSIA information can be obtained
at www.ICGtesting.com
Printed in the USA
LVHW041941071020
668213LV00009B/1374